Do it The Lazy Way

1. Pay cash and pay full balances.

2. If you can't stop using it, put a Post-It® on your credit card and record purchases each time you "charge it" to keep track of how much you're spending.

3. Set an egg timer by the phone when you make long-distance calls to keep from talking too long.

4. Mark bill due dates on your calendar so you pay them on time and avoid costly late charges, interest, and other penalty fees.

5. Join the city or community gym or a recreational sports team instead of paying pricey health club dues.

*One luxurious
bubble bath*

*Access to most comfortable
chair and favorite TV show*

*One half-hour massage
(will need to recruit spouse, child, friend)*

*Time to recline and listen to a favorite CD
(or at least one song)*

cut

Do it **The Lazy Way**
alpha books

6. Savor a cheap but elegant lunch. Pack a brown paper bag with leftover lasagna from last night's dinner, a linen napkin, and silver cutlery. If it's sunny, eat alfresco at the local park. Just like Tuscany!

7. Instead of paying your mortgage once a month, divide the amount in half and pay it every two weeks. You'll shave at least six years off a 30-year loan and save hundreds of thousands of dollars in interest.

8. Improve your bottom line and your bottom. Walk, bike, or in-line skate to work instead of taking the car.

9. Love chic clothes but can't afford the prices? Shop at sample sales, where designers sell prototypes of their new lines for as little as 10 percent of what the items will cost at department stores and upscale boutiques.

10. Forget price tags and beware of coupons. Read unit costs on the super-market shelves to get the best deals.

The Lazy Way
alpha books

COUPON

The Lazy Way
alpha books

COUPON

The Lazy Way
alpha books

COUPON

The Lazy Way
alpha books

COUPON

cut

Cut
Your
Spending

The Lazy Way™

Cut Your Spending

Leslie Haggin

The Lazy Way™

Macmillan • USA

To Mummy, Sean, and Dad—For their love and encouragement, and of course, for spoiling me with lovely dinners when I was tackling debts of my own.

Macmillan Publishing books may be purchased for business or sales promotional use. For information please write: Special Markets Department, Macmillan Publishing USA, 1633 Broadway, New York, NY 10019.

International Standard Book Number: 0-02-863002-5
Library of Congress Catalog Card Number: 98-89534

01 00 99   8 7 6 5 4 3 2 1

Interpretation of the printing code: the rightmost number of the first series of numbers is the year of the book's printing; the rightmost number of the second series of numbers is the number of the book's printing. For example, a printing code of 99-1 shows that the first printing occurred in 1999.

Printed in the United States of America

Book Design: Madhouse Studios

Page Creation: David Faust, Lisa England, and Heather Pope.

You Don't Have to Feel Guilty Anymore!

IT'S O.K. TO DO IT *THE LAZY WAY*!

It seems every time we turn around, we're given more responsibility, more information to absorb, more places we need to go, and more numbers, dates, and names to remember. Both our bodies and our minds are already on overload. And we know what happens next—cleaning the house, balancing the checkbook, and cooking dinner get put off until "tomorrow" and eventually fall by the wayside.

So let's be frank—we're all starting to feel a bit guilty about the dirty laundry, stacks of ATM slips, and Chinese takeout. Just thinking about tackling those terrible tasks makes you exhausted, right? If only there were an easy, effortless way to get this stuff done! (And done right!)

There is—*The Lazy Way*! By providing the pain-free way to do something—including tons of shortcuts and timesaving tips, as well as lists of all the stuff you'll ever need to get it done efficiently—*The Lazy Way* series cuts through all of the time-wasting thought processes and laborious exercises. You'll discover the secrets of those who have figured out *The Lazy Way*. You'll get things done in half the time it takes the average person—and then you will sit back and smugly consider those poor suckers who haven't discovered *The Lazy Way* yet. With *The Lazy Way,* you'll learn how to put in minimal effort and get maximum results so you can devote your attention and energy to the pleasures in life!

THE LAZY WAY PROMISE

Everyone on *The Lazy Way* staff promises that, if you adopt *The Lazy Way* philosophy, you'll never break a sweat, you'll barely lift a finger, you won't put strain on your brain, and you'll have plenty of time to put up your feet. We guarantee you will find that these activities are no longer hardships, since you're doing them *The Lazy Way*. We also firmly support taking breaks and encourage rewarding yourself (we even offer our suggestions in each book!). With *The Lazy Way*, the only thing you'll be overwhelmed by is all of your newfound free time!

THE LAZY WAY SPECIAL FEATURES

Every book in our series features the following sidebars in the margins, all designed to save you time and aggravation down the road.

- **"Quick 'n' Painless"**—shortcuts that get the job done fast.

- **"You'll Thank Yourself Later"**—advice that saves time down the road.

- **"A Complete Waste of Time"**—warnings that spare countless headaches and squandered hours.

- **"If You're So Inclined"**—optional tips for moments of inspired added effort.

- **"The Lazy Way"**—rewards to make the task more pleasurable.

If you've either decided to give up altogether or have taken a strong interest in the subject, you'll find information on hiring outside help with "How to Get Someone Else to Do It" as well as further reading recommendations in "If You Want to Learn More, Read These." In addition, there's an only-what-you-need-to-know glossary of terms and product names ("If You Don't Know What It Means/Does, Look Here") as well as "It's Time for Your Reward"—fun and relaxing ways to treat yourself for a job well done.

With *The Lazy Way* series, you'll find that getting the job done has never been so painless!

Series Editor
Amy Gordon

Editorial Director
Gary Krebs

Director of Creative Services
Michele Laseau

Cover Designer
Michael Freeland

Managing Editor
Robert Shuman

Development Editor
Maureen Horn

Production Editor
Mark Enochs

What's in This Book

If You Feel Your Spending Is Out of Control, It's Time to Make the Cut

It's well past midnight, but you're wide awake worrying about all the money you owe: credit cards, medical bills, unpaid taxes, student loans—even the Girl Scouts are charging you interest for boxes of unpaid Thin Mints. And it's all because you can't seem to budget your money in a way that fits your lifestyle.

You'd love to pay everyone. It's embarrassing that your German Shepherd, Sid Vicious, wags his tail and licks the now all-too-familiar collection agent at your door. Then there's that pretty lady at the supermarket who used to be so nice about giving you free cheese samples until you had a small cocktail party in Aisle 5. Were you hearing things, or did she really call you a "deadbeat" when you asked if she had a second party platter?

The truth is, as much as you want to do the right thing, you can't get out of debt when you're broke. If you had the cash, you wouldn't be in this jam, now would you?

Wrong!!!

Getting out of debt and learning to cut your spending may take time and discipline, but it isn't impossible, and it doesn't mean you have to live like a Trappist monk to do it.

The first step is to stop getting angry at yourself. Mea culpas won't pay your bills. And stop feeling humiliated. It's no fun being in debt, but you're not alone. Last year, a record 1.4 million Americans filed for bankruptcy protection. And sixty percent of our nation's households are burdened with credit-card debts averaging more than $7,000.

Don't completely blame yourself. Experts like Stephen Brobeck, executive director of the Consumer Federation of America, says people aren't lazy about paying what they owe. He blames banks and other lenders who stand to make millions of dollars by getting consumers in over their heads, and then profiting on interest, penalty fees, and late charges. If you don't believe this, think about the following.

Last year, more than 3.1 billion (yes, that's a *b*) credit-card solicitations were mailed to American homes. That's roughly 30 per household, offering such perks as bargain-basement interest rates, free vacations, or merchandise. (You got that desk set, too?) But does anyone talk about the fine print: bogus grace periods, retroactive interest, and other hidden fees?

Now you're getting the idea.

A savvy debt-buster looks beyond the come-ons and reads the fine print. And you don't have to be a Mensa member or have lots of time to avoid common and costly traps. Each day there are plenty of opportunities to save a bundle on costs you can't avoid: meals, household expenses, utility bills, transportation, health care. Even sending your kid to college doesn't have to require getting a loan from the International Monetary Fund.

Cutting out extras doesn't have to be painful, either. In fact, chances are you have a lot more to gain than extra cash by cutting back. There are friends to barter with and new skills to acquire when you stop paying expensive contractors. You'll probably get healthier by using your feet instead of taxis and do more for your heart by dining in than hitting the take-out windows. And admit it, as smart as you are, reading a good book from the library instead of spending $25 on a small popcorn and Coke at the local movie theater could do your old brain some good, too.

Why not start with this book? After all, you have a lot to gain by learning how to be wise with your hard-earned money.

THANK YOU...

This book would not have been written without the encouragement, good humor, sound counsel of Andree Abecassis, the world's best agent. Editors Maureen Horn and Amy Gordon kept me on track with patient editorial support. And of course, much gratitude to Robert Geary, who provided a decent computer on which to work, sanity and assistance when I hit the delete key—and when chapters were finished—the reward of fine conversation, a run, or a cold beer. Thanks to you all!

Quickly Control Credit and Cash Flow

Are you too lazy to read Quickly Control Credit and Cash Flow?

1 Sure, you've got a solid spending plan. Withdraw $20 bills from the automated bank teller until there are no more left. ☐ yes ☐ no

2 Refinancing is what you do each time you ask friends and family for more money to pay the rent. ☐ yes ☐ no

3 You have a 13 percent fixed-rate mortgage. The bad news: Rates have fallen by half since you got your loan in the early 1980s. The good news: The fixed rate gives you something you can rely on. ☐ yes ☐ no

Taking Stock of What You Have, What You Owe, and What They Say About You in Your Credit Report

You're lost in the middle of the forest. What do you do?

a) Panic.

b) Walk in circles and sing tunes from your favorite Broadway musicals.

c) Look at a trail map to figure out where you are.

Of course you go for the map and leave show tunes for another day. Well, dealing with debt is exactly like getting back on the forest trail after getting lost somewhere between Devil's Mountain and Great Gulch Gorge.

Don't believe me? Be honest. Don't those stacks of bills, that ever-growing pile of collection notices, and the overdue parking tickets you stuffed under the passenger seat of your Dodge Dart make you feel a little lost? Doesn't being so disorganized make you fret just a little?

Here's the good news. With a minimum amount of effort, you can get organized, figure out what you owe, what you have, and how good or bad your credit is so you can get back on track.

Why bother? Don't you want to see the peaks and valleys instead of dead-ends and pitfalls? Wouldn't you rather get home, where it's warm and comfy, rather than waiting it out in the middle of nowhere?

I thought so.

COMMAND CENTRAL: WHERE THE GOOD, THE NOT-SO-GOOD, AND THE WAY-PAST-DUE COME TOGETHER

Must-Have Equipment

- Desk or quiet place to work where kids, dog, roommates, or other wildlife won't disturb you
- Comfortable chair (but stay away from Lay-Z-Boys)
- Light (with working bulb) so you can see what you're doing
- File cabinet
- Files
- File holders or accordion file holder (in lieu of cabinet)

- Blank adhesive labels for files
- Paper
- Paper Clips
- Stapler
- Sharpened pencils
- Colored pens
- Wall calendar
- Writing tools (Benedictine monk with quill and vellum, typewriter, or computer with printer will do. Take your pick.)

Other Important Stuff:

- Tax return
- Warranties (for everything from the toaster to the Toyota)
- Credit report (more on this later)
- Store receipts

Must-Get Bills

Note: These will be listed by different categories!
Household:

- Mortgage
- Rent stubs
- Homeowners' or renters' insurance
- Property tax bill
- Household services like cleaning service, pool cleaner, and so on

Gathering your financial records together doesn't have to be boring. Turn on your favorite record— Wagner's *Ring Cycle*, the Sex Pistols, James Brown—and sing along as you gather your bills in one place.

The Lazy Way

Utility Bills:

- Phone
- Water
- Electricity
- Gas
- Services, such as the bill for plumber who was called to your house on Christmas Eve when the pipes burst

Food:

- Supermarket receipts
- Bills from restaurant, caterer, liquor store, and so on
- Credit-card bills (bank and charge cards, too): Visa, American Express, MasterCard, department store charge cards, Diner's Club, gasoline charge cards

Education:

- Tuition
- Student-loan agreement/payment schedule
- Charges from campus bookstore

Medical:

- Doctors' bills
- Medical insurance or HMO payments
- Life insurance
- Invoice from pharmacy
- Hospital emergency room invoice
- Health club dues

Transportation:

- Automobile loan
- Lease agreement payment schedule
- Insurance
- Mechanic bill
- Parking, traffic, speeding tickets
- Tolls
- Commuter pass receipt

Entertainment/Holiday:

- Bills from record store, charges for concert tickets, bookstore, and so on
- Bills for newspaper home-delivery
- Cable television bill
- Payment schedule for large-screen TV you bought just before the Super Bowl

Pet/Misc.:

- Unpaid vet, dog-groomer, cat-trainer bills
- IOUs to friends and family
- Collection agency notices

Must-Get Receipts

There are probably many things you buy that you don't get a bill for. Gather any receipts you have, or start saving receipts, for things like grocery bills, the book-store, and the dry cleaners. File those receipts with bills according to their category. They will be handy when it comes to planning a personal budget.

YOU'LL THANK YOURSELF LATER

You're doing a great job gathering your bills in one place. Eventually, you're going to have to sort them. Why not get a head start? As you bring them back to your desk or other designated work station, drop them off in piles according to their type: house bills, entertainment, medical, and so on. You'll be one step ahead of the game when it comes time to sorting through what you owe.

Keeping bills in separate files according to their category is a great way to keep them from getting lost among ponderous stacks of paper. Why not assign colors to help you identify what's what even more quickly? For example, use a red marker to label *Automobile* for your car costs. Blue for *Household*. Green for *Medical*. Use the same colors when you mark *paid* on the bills. Color-coding bills also helps ensure they won't get filed incorrectly.

Gather The Best for Last:

Your Income and Assets:

- Pay stubs
- Checking account (and old stubs from the past year)
- Savings account
- Securities: stocks, bonds, mutual funds
- IRA (Individual Retirement Account) or Keogh plan statements
- 401(k)
- Life insurance (its value if you cashed it in today)

PUTTING IT ALL AWAY

Now that you've pulled your bills and other papers together, it's time to sort them. There's no right or wrong way to organize what you have, but there are a few rules to make it easier to stay focused.

1. Use a system that's easy for you to use and, most important, to maintain. There's no use getting organized only to let everything turn chaotic again.

2. Organize bills by type or category.

3. Organize expenses chronologically so you don't lose a current bill among the invoices you paid years ago.

4. Stay visual. Use a file cabinet or accordion files. Stacks of papers tend to get shuffled and mixed up. That means no more stuffing bills in old shoe boxes or shopping bags.

5. Clearly label all files.

Heck, if you have old bills you've paid, celebrate your past responsibility. Don't just toss them out; have a purging ceremony. Dim the lights. Light candles. Chant, "Be gone! Be gone!" as you drop those tired, old papers into the trash. Feel free!

PUTTING YOUR BILLS AWAY STEP-BY-STEP

1. Separate bills by category.

2. Go through the category and separate paid from unpaid bills.

3. Bills you paid years ago can get thrown out. (Hooray!)

4. Bills you paid but want to keep, mark *Paid* in bold, clear writing.

5. File the bills that are paid. Put the oldest ones in the back of a clearly labeled file (for example, *Car Bills—Paid*), the more current invoices at the front of your file.

6. Go through bills that need to be paid. If something is late, write *late.* Bills that need to be paid in the future, write *due*, or circle the due date so you can easily spot when it needs to be paid.

7. File bills that need to be paid.

Is your student loan due the 15th of every month? Don't trust yourself to remember. Mark all 12 months on your calendar. When sporadic bills (Bloomingdale's charge for your friend's wedding gift) arrive in the mail,

A COMPLETE WASTE OF TIME

The 3 Worst Things to Do When Sorting Through Bills:

1. Save the box of cancelled checks you wrote a decade ago.

2. Frame the bills you did pay, and then hang them in your den as proof that you're "not so irresponsible" after all.

3. Keep notices from the collection agency next to your voodoo doll so you can "show them a thing or two" about pestering you for payment.

open them immediately and mark the due date on your calendar if you can't pay it immediately. Then file the bill in your *Due* or *To Be Paid* files.

Oh yeah, hang the calendar where you'll see it.

EVERYTHING YOU NEED TO KNOW ABOUT CREDIT REPORTS BUT DIDN'T THINK TO ASK

You gather your bills, you know when they're due, and you have a tidy file filled with warrantees, bank statements, and other financial data. But what about the stuff you pushed aside years ago? The late student-loan payments. The year you never paid a single charge-card bill on time. How badly is your past haunting you today? Credit reports are a great way for you to find out whether or not you ruined your chances on taking out a loan for that villa in the south of France.

Even if you're not planning to borrow soon, everyone should look at their credit reports because they're used to determine if you can qualify for bank cards, insurance, if you can rent a home, or even get a job.

And many reports are riddled with mistakes.

Nearly one-third of all reports contained "serious errors" such as false delinquencies or accounts that belong to other consumers, according to a study by Public Interest Research Group. Whether you owe a lot or just won the lottery, there's no reason for you to shoulder the burden of false information that can affect you for years.

Fortunately, it's not difficult, and it may even be free, to find out if your credit report is accurate and to take steps to make corrections.

Where Can I Get My Credit Report?

There are three major credit-reporting agencies in the United States:

Equifax

P.O. Box 740241

Atlanta, GA 30374

To order a credit report: (800) 685-1111

Web address: www.equifax.com/

Trans Union

P.O. Box 390

Springfield, PA 19064-0390

To order a credit report: (800) 916-8800

Web address: www.tuc.com/

Experian

P.O. Box 1017

Allen, TX 75013

To order a credit report: (800) 682-7654

Web address: www.experian.com/personal.htm

How Much Do Credit Reports Cost?

Credit reports cost up to $8 with a few notable exceptions. New Jersey, Vermont, Maryland, Massachusetts, Colorado, Connecticut, Maine, and Georgia cap the price for their state residents at less than $8, and reports may even be free.

IF YOU'RE SO INCLINED

It's a good idea to file bills that are due and those that have been paid in separate places. (If nothing else, it keeps you honest about what's really been paid.) You can use different drawers in a file cabinet or separate accordion files. Label the cabinet doors or the accordion files with stickers: *Paid Bills* and *To Be Paid*. When you pay a bill, mark paid on the bill and move it from the unpaid files into the paid file.

Free reports must be given to anyone who is unemployed and will look for work within 60 days, welfare recipients, anyone who has been denied credit, anyone who thinks he or she is the victim of fraud or identity theft.

The Federal Trade Commission has a few websites where you can get free information about the Fair Credit Reporting Act with just a few clicks on your computer keyboard.

The agency's main website address is: www.ftc.gov.

Also, check out the Trade Commission's easy-to-read summary of the Fair Credit Reporting Act: www.ftc.gov/bcp/conline/edcams/fcra/index.html

WHAT DO I NEED TO DO TO GET MY REPORT BY MAIL?

There are a few key items you must include in your request for a credit report. They are:

1. Your full name, including Sr. or III, and so on

2. Your Social Security number

3. Your full address and any former addresses if you moved within the past five years

4. Proof of residency, such as a copy of a utility bill (not a definite, but may be requested)

5. Your spouse's full name

6. Phone number(s) where you can be reached

7. The address of where you want your report mailed

IF YOU'RE SO
INCLINED

In 1996, Congress passed the Fair Credit Reporting Act giving consumers rights to obtain and control what goes into their reports. It's easy to know more about your rights in dealing with reporting agencies and creditors who supply information about you.

8. Check for the cost of your report or a clearly stated reason why you are asking for a free report

9. Don't forget to sign the letter

Your request should be simple and to the point. Just ask for the report and include the above information.

Things You'll Find in Your Credit Report:

- Your name
- Birthdate
- Social Security number
- Address and previous addresses for past five years
- Names of your employer(s)
- Accounts
- Your credit limits
- Loans, including the amount and type (student loan, mortgage, automobile)
- Defaults on any loans
- Lawsuit judgments
- Payment history, including late payments
- Anyone who has asked for your credit report

Okay, let's see if you get this right: All information on credit reports is deleted after seven years. True or False?____

If you answered False, treat yourself to an ice cream sundae. Most information stays on reports for seven years, but serious violations, like bankruptcies or loan defaults, may stay on a report for up to 10 years.

IF YOU'RE SO INCLINED

Credit reports can vary depending on who's issuing them. If you're writing or calling, why not do two or write all three agencies? Even if you have to spend $8 for the report, it may be well worth it to cover your tracks and know what's being said about you before someone else does.

QUICK ⬤ PAINLESS

What Do I Do If I Disagree with My Report?

Unlike family members who never listen to you, credit-reporting agencies must verify any information you dispute within 30 days or get rid of it. (Thank the Fair Credit Reporting Act for that one.)

If you disagree with information on your report, write the credit-reporting agency and/or the creditor that supplied the information (the bank, retail stores, and so on) and ask for a correction.

When you write the letter, be simple and to-the-point. For example, you may find an account listed on your report that you closed years ago. Simply write that you closed the account and want it removed. If you have documentation to support your claim, include it. Include personal information listed above (name, Social Security number, and so on) that you used when you asked for the report.

What Happens If They Don't Fix a Mistake?

Don't despair! As a consumer, you have a right to keep fighting to clear your good name. If you and the credit-reporting agency continue to disagree, you may:

1. File a statement in your credit report as to why you disagree with the report. Anyone who checks your report will see it.

2. File a complaint against the credit-reporting agency. Contact the Federal Trade Commission at:

6th and Pennsylvania Avenues, NW

Washington, DC 20580

(202) 326-2222

The FTC has regional offices throughout the United States, and it may be easier to seek help closer to home. Check the agency's website (see above for e-mail address) for a listing of offices nearest to you.

3. Take legal action by suing either a creditor or credit-reporting agency.

Additional Resources:

Public Interest Research Group

218 D St., SE

Washington, DC 20003

(203) 546-9707

http://pirg.org/consumer/credit/

PIRG's website has fantastic resources on consumer rights guaranteed under the Fair Credit Reporting Act plus more how-to advice on dealing with credit-reporting agencies.

National Foundation for

Consumer Credit Counseling Service

8611 Second Ave. No. 100

Silver Spring, MD 20910

(800) 388-2227

Additional Reading:

Credit Repair Kit, Third Edition, by John Ventura, Dearborn Financial Publishing, Inc., Chicago, IL

It's not fun battling credit-reporting agencies to clear your record. Reward yourself by spending time in more supportive environments. Call your mother and have her feed you gingersnaps and hot chocolate. That doesn't work? Call your buddy, girlfriend, or the family dog and ask them to spoil you with a drink, a cuddle, or a slobbery kiss on the cheek.

The Lazy Way

Getting Money on Your Side

	The Old Way	**The Lazy Way**
Getting your credit report	You use your mom as a reference	You order a credit report
Dealing with bills	You search in the recycling bin hoping you didn't throw out the utility bill	Everything is in your file cabinet, organized by bills' due dates
Paying debts on time	When the collection agent shows up at your door, you know it's time to pay	You have a calendar in your study marked with the dates that your rent and other bills are due

Building a Budget That Will Get You Out of Debt

You know all about budgets. They're complex tabulations, plans, and flow charts for rich people like your neighbor who made a bundle on securities. (You thought she was talking about dead bolts and burglar alarms.) But you? You owe a lot, and you have a little. What could you possibly budget?

Plenty.

A budget is ideal for anyone trying to make ends meet. It allows you to track where you're spending all your money and where you can trim costs. By planning expenses wisely, you can make a schedule to pay off your debt, save for emergencies, pay for small rewards, and save for long-term goals like that dream retirement cottage in the English countryside.

Does this sound familiar? Budget = Boring. No Fun. Rain on Saturday. Hate to say it, but your attitude is probably one reason you can't get yourself to budget your expenses. Try thinking about a budget as something different, something positive. How to do that? Pick a euphemism. It's fast, easy, and free. Instead of using the word budget, think of a personal spending plan, a fiscal road map, your private insurance policy against debt, a safety lock on your hard-earned cash. There's nothing a good euphemism can't fix. Just ask the guy who decided he was downsized instead of fired.

YOU WON'T NEED A COMPASS, BUT A CALCULATOR WILL DO—TOOLS FOR CHARTING A BUDGET

- Calculator
- Pencil with eraser (because even you make mistakes)
- Old bills and list of expenses
- List of your income (See Part 3 for details or expenses and income)

Pick one of the following:

- Accountant ledger book
- Legal-sized paper
- Computer budgeting software (if you want to use the computer)

Do-Ahead Organizing

A budget is a plan of what you can spend and what you'll earn during a fixed amount or "window" of time. That said, you need to base your budget on blocks of time that are the most manageable for you. Some people find it easy to budget according to their pay schedule or by monthly installments. Daily budgets are too short a time frame. A yearly budget is too large, too, although you should have long-term goals built into your budget that may take more than a year to achieve.

The next thing to keep in mind is that making a budget is like dancing. Once you master a few simple steps, you can sail through life with the lightness of knowing you're not wasting your money. We'll go into detail about each step, but in general, you will:

1. List your income.

2. List your current expenses.

3. List and calculate the total cost of all unpaid debts.

4. Organize expenses by fixed costs (those that can't be avoided, like rent) and optional or flexible expenditures (food, movie tickets, green nail polish).

5. If must-pay bills are less than your income, budget the unused portion for flexible costs, debts, occasional treats, savings.

6. If must-pay bills are more than your income, you need to make radical changes (like getting a new job or moving in with family until you catch your breath financially); otherwise, you'll keep getting into debt.

Step One: List Your Income

If you pulled together your assets and other bills (see chapter 1), then you're ahead of the game. On a piece of paper, in a ledger, or on your computer, list the type of income in one column and what it's worth for whatever time period you choose. Income could be everything from stock dividends, Social Security, salaries, rent from your boarder, allowance, tax rebate, and so on. A sample for a single month's budgeting could look like this:

A COMPLETE WASTE OF TIME

The 3 Worst Things You Can Do When Trying to Budget Your Money:

1. Plan your budgets on a daily basis.

2. Keep the oldest debts in the back of your bill pile. Pay the new ones first.

3. Don't bother saving old checks.

Salary	$3,400
Checking Account	$450
Savings Account	$700
Stock Dividends	
Apex Co.	$70
XYZ Corp.	$0
Total	$4,620

Step Two: List Your Expenses

Remember those bills you organized by category (see chapter 1)? It's time to look at them to see where you spend your money. Expenses could be things like:

Household: rent, gas, water, phone, insurance

Car: insurance, tolls, gas, repairs

Medical: monthly heart pills, glasses

Entertainment: health club fees, movies, restaurant

List expenses, plus costs, for the time period of your budget. For example, a month's entry could look like this: Fixed Costs:

Rent	$850
Utilities	$160
Child care	$450
Student loan	$200
Total	$1,660

Flexible Costs:

Groceries	$250
Restaurants	$100
Commuter rail pass	$60
Clothing	$150
Fun	$150
Health club	$45
Savings set aside	$200
Charity	$15
Other	$200
Debt	TO BE FILLED IN LATER
Total	$1,170
Fix/Flex Total	$2,830

Step Three: Figure Out Costs of All Your Debts

There are expenses you owe this month, like the phone bill. Then there are the bills that have dogged you for years, like the student loan, credit-card bill, and car lease you can't seem to pay off. Tally your outstanding bills, look at collection notices, and check your credit report (see chapter 1) to gauge what you owe and how much. Is the total $5,000? $15,000? More than that? Don't panic. You need to identify the beast before you can slay it. Once you know how much you owe, you can build in

YOU'LL THANK YOURSELF LATER

As you look through your overdue expenses, notice which ones are costing you the most money. Look at interest, penalty fees, and late charges (they're usually the small print on the bottom or back of your bill). What you pay could vary drastically. For example, the balance on one credit-card bill could carry a 7.9 percent interest rate, while another might charge you a whopping 21 percent. When it comes time to paying debts, you'll want to pay off bills with the most expensive interest and penalty fees first.

payments as part of your regular budget cycle. Knowing what you owe, compared to what you earn, also will make you assess if you need to make more drastic changes, like getting a more lucrative job.

Step Four: Compare Your Costs Versus Income

Add your monthly costs and your income. If you have anything left over, you're in good shape. You can use surplus to pay outstanding bills. Factor in how much you can set aside to paying debt on a regular basis. You might do this by thinking about how long it will take to get rid of your debt. If you want to pay all of your overdue bills by the end of the year, divide what you owe by 12 and see if you can afford to pay steady payments each month. If you pay twice as much, you could get rid of the bills in six months.

Remember, you aren't just paying the original bill (principle), you also must pay interest and other fees. Because of this, the longer you take to pay bills, the more it costs in excess fees. Repeat this mantra over and over again. Pay debt slowly = more expensive to get rid of. Pay debt faster = cheaper for you.

A NOTE OF ENCOURAGEMENT

Living on an allowance doesn't mean you can't have fun. It just keeps you from diving in over your head even if you enjoy modest splurges. It's like that bottle of delicious Merlot just in from Napa Valley. You love wine, but it costs $25. You can buy it. Just remember if you took out $100 for the week, you only have $75 left. This means you'll have to give up other things that aren't as important to you to stay within that budget. It might be easier to do than you think.

How about those $5 super-jumbo-combo-value meals from Burgers-R-Us? Brown bag a sandwich instead of buying your midday meal, and you've made up for the wine without too much effort at all. Besides, everyone knows it's a faux pas to drink a decent bottle of wine with food that comes from a drive-through window.

Step Five: Dealing with Debt When It's Bigger Than Your Income

There's no way to get around it, but if you earn less than what you currently owe, you'll only increase your debt. You'll have to rein in costs and/or increase your income. This may mean you need a raise, a new job, or part-time work until you catch up.

The Perils of Not Budgeting for Emergencies as Shown in the Tale of a Dog and a Chicken Bone

You're working so hard to pay your bills and make ends meet that setting aside money for emergencies is out of the question. Reconsider this. Emergency funds can save you money in the long run. Remember when your Golden Retriever swallowed a chicken bone, and it got lodged in her throat? You had no money set aside for unexpected pitfalls, and you charged the $250 vet bill. That was a year ago. You pay minimum balances, but with the card's 18 percent annual interest, you now have a bill that's ballooned to $295, not including late fees for those months you can't pay on time. Yikes!

QUICK ⬛ PAINLESS

Sticking to the most carefully thought-out spending plans can be difficult if you keep withdrawing money from your account or writing checks. Pay yourself a weekly allowance, say $100 cash, and don't let yourself have any more. Take your automated bank teller or debit card out of your wallet and leave the checkbook at home so you don't cheat.

Generally, you should set aside three to six months worth of living expenses. If you don't have that much at hand, contribute to your emergency stash by setting aside a fixed amount on a regular basis.

If saving three to six months costs still seems harder than flying to the moon, set aside something. It's a good habit to get into, and you may be able to stave off the small fiascoes. You probably can come up with $20 a month without much effort. That's worth the cost of the $1 you spend every weekday morning on a cup of coffee or $240 after a year. Now don't you wish you had done that before the dog ate your drumstick?

Short-Cut Cost Cuts

What do you spend your money on without thinking? The following are mindless purchases we all make. Convenience goods and services—such as low-cost take-out dinners when you're too tired to cook, maid service, or taxi cabs—can do the most damage to your wallet. Think about what you're paying for. Is it worth it?

> Four take-out dinners a week:
> $13 per meal, $52 per week, $208 per month, $ 2,496 per year

> Monday to Friday doughnut and plain black coffee:
> $1.50 per day, $7.50 per week, $30 per month, $360 per year

> Saturday night drinks with friends at the local pub:
> $20 per outing, $80 per month, $1,040 per year or 52 Saturdays

Jack Kerouac. Mother Theresa. Jewel. What do they have in common? Well, they all struggled with money during the course of their lives. If you just confirmed that you're living beyond your means (your job isn't cutting it), call on a friend, family, or talk to the cat, and ask them to list your sparkling attributes. Listen carefully to their praise and get excited for finding a new job, asking for a raise, or doing a little moonlighting. Some of the world's most talented people have been in your slightly worn-out shoes. You will get out of debt!

The Lazy Way

Pack of cigarettes a day:

$2.50 a pack, $17.50 a week, $70 a month, $910 a year

Bimonthly house cleaning service:

$40 a cleaning, $80 a month, $960 a year

Top-Ten Hits: the two compact discs you buy a month:

$13 a CD, $26 a month, $312 a year

Three taxi cab rides a month:

$10 per ride, $30 per month, $360 per year

FOLLOW-UP FINANCIAL PLANNING

Keeping a budget gets easier with time because you get to know your spending habits. Keep track of what you spend when you first start your budget. Is your clothes allowance too large? Did you spend twice as much on groceries as you planned?

Set aside receipts or record your purchases in a notebook to help you gauge what you spend. After a while, you won't need to check up on yourself so often.

Don't binge-budget. It's like binge dieting, and the gains you make one month will be spent the next. Budget if your expenses shoot up. Unforeseen expenses, such as the new generator for your old Volvo, are a pain. But don't let them stall you. Hit your emergency fund or figure out how you can pay it off each month. Keeping your cool will help you from giving up.

Budget if your income rises. It's easy to feel like spending when we have more. What happens when you

IF YOU'RE SO INCLINED

Even if you have the most unsinkable budget, there could be leaks. To keep from becoming a financial Titanic, carry a little notebook or index card with you at all times and jot down all your expenses. You'll be surprised to see how quickly the little purchases accumulate. That money could be used for paying off your debt.

win $100 playing bingo, or your family gives you birthday money, the tax return arrives, you get a raise, or you pay off all of your bills? Do you go nuts and buy a new wardrobe or a new stereo?

Budget the surplus for emergencies, long-term goals, or investments and try to use just a bit for more modest rewards, like one outfit or a concert ticket. After all, you deserve the extra cash, but that doesn't mean there won't be leaner times ahead.

Getting Money on Your Side

	The Old Way	The Lazy Way
Living on a budget	"What's a ?" budget	If you don't have time to count pennies, set aside a fixed amount of cash you can spend in a week, and don't take out extra. You'll avoid wiping out your nest egg.
Paying for emergencies	Pay for all unforseen costs with credit cards and then hide the bill when it arrives.	Take a bit of cash from your pay checks on a regular basis and put it into an emergency fund.
Rent	Hide from landlord until you have rent money.	No problem. You know when it's due and you've budgeted extra month's rent in a special account so you never get caught short.

Part 2

Simply Squash Those Sneaky Little Fees

Are you too lazy to read Simply Squash Those Sneaky Little Fees?

1 Flathead and Phillips. Fitting nicknames for bad boyfriends you'd rather forget. ☐ yes ☐ no

2 The microwave you use to heat your Hungry Man dinners broke, and you haven't eaten for a week. ☐ yes ☐ no

3 You've asked for so many free cosmetic samples that your picture is posted at the department store makeup counter with a big warning sign. No more free exfoliant! No more mascara! ☐ yes ☐ no

Chapter three

How to Make Sure Your Bank Doesn't Rob You

In the old days, robbers like Jesse James galloped into town, blew up the bank, kicked back a few shots of whiskey, and then galloped into the distance with sacks of money.

These days, it seems the robbers are in the banks. They're better dressed, though, with their tailored suits and friendly smiles. Then all of a sudden, they tell you that you need to deposit the gross national product of a small island nation to earn any interest at all on your savings. They charge you for each check you write (not to mention the checks themselves), attach surcharges if you use your debit card at ATMs that do and don't belong to them, and make you pay fees if you speak to one of their tellers over the phone.

We don't realize we're being robbed because the fees we pay seem minimal. Two dollars here. A buck thirty there. Little bites are easy for consumers to swallow. In fact, half of all bank customers would tolerate a 50-cent ATM increase to $2 per transaction, up from $1.50, according to one survey by Mentis Corporation, which surveys banks.

Yet, so-called nominal banking expenses are costing all of us more than a vault of cash. Banks made $18 billion on fees in 1997. Even Jesse James could have used some of that to pay his bar tab. Think about how you could use the amount your bank is taking for "services" on debts, investments, education, or making at least one or two lifelong dreams come true.

The plethora of bank mergers may make it difficult to find refuge from many of these costs. But it's not impossible to find ways to keep the bank from getting its hands on your money. Savvy consumers know what to ask banks so they can make sure that when they deposit their hard-earned cash, it stays in their account. After all, isn't that why you stopped tucking your savings under your mattress?

BOUNCING IS BAD FOR YOUR BUDGET

It seems like it would be a no-brainer. Don't write a check if you don't have the cash. Funny how the simplest rules are tough to follow.

Americans in 1997 shelled out more than $5 billion in penalty fees for writing bad checks. That's a ton of cash, especially when the average fee for a bounced check was $17.39 at banks and $15.42 at credit unions.

Where do we all go so wrong? Clue: It's not your upbringing. But careless record keeping may be costing you unnecessary expenses.

Most of us are vigilant about recording all of our check transactions. But are you as careful to deduct withdrawals you make from your account with an ATM or debit card? Taking a few seconds to record all of your withdrawals (and deposits) will keep your balance current and accurate, so you can avoid writing bad checks.

Warning! It could cost you to cash that check. U.S. Public Interest Research Group has found that some banks now charge their own customers if they deposit someone else's bad check! Ask your bank if you're liable for these deposit-item-return fees. You may want to take your business elsewhere if this is the case.

QUESTIONS TO ASK BEFORE YOU OPEN THAT BANK ACCOUNT

All banks charge fees of some sort, but some charge less than others. The Consumer Federation of America and other watchdog groups advise that smaller branches and credit unions will cost you less than the 300 "big" banks that control nearly 75 percent of all deposits. (There are roughly 9,000 banks nationwide.)

It's probably a good idea if you choose three to five local banks or credit unions and ask them what fees they charge (and how much they are) before you decide where to deposit your money.

YOU'LL THANK YOURSELF LATER

1. Minimum balance: Do you need to keep a minimum balance to avoid penalty charges? Some banks increase interest payments if you deposit more money. What is the minimum amount you need to keep to earn the best interest possible? Do you pay any fines if your balance goes below the minimum requirement?

If you don't carry your check register with you, keep a Post-It® on your bank card and write down the date and amount of any withdrawal or deposit you make, and then record it in your check register to keep accurate balance information.

2. Foreign or Off-Use Fees: These are fees you pay if you use automated-teller machines that belong to another bank. The average surcharge fee in 1998 is $1.18. (Big banks charged $1.32 on average. Small banks charged $1.12, and credit unions charged 80 cents.) Does your bank charge surcharge fees? How much is it?

3. Surcharges: These are fees other banks charge you if you use their automated-teller machine, and you're not one of their customers. The average surcharge in 1998 is $1.23, up from $1.15 a year before. Be forewarned! Many banks don't post warnings that you're about to pay a surcharge. Connecticut, Iowa, and Massachusetts ban surcharges.

4. ATM Transaction Fees: That handy machine that lets you get money 24 hours a day may cost you, even if you do use your bank's machine. Does your bank or credit union charge transaction fees? How much are they?

5. Cashier's Checks, Certified Checks, Money Orders: How much do they cost? Post offices sometimes charge less for money orders.

6. Stop Payment: Oops. You paid your electric bill twice, so you call and ask your bank to stop payment on the second check. Think twice about that one. Stop payment fees are hefty: more the $15 at most banks. It might be better to get credit from the electric company instead.

7. Human Teller Fees: You want to find out if a check has cleared or if you have any money left, so you call the bank's handy 800 information number. Hate to tell you, but chances are that call isn't free. Banks often charge fees for speaking with a real live human who can quickly answer your questions. Fees usually run about $1. Try keeping your bank balance up to date or use automated systems (the ones where you have to punch numbers and the star-key on your phone pad).

IT'S NOT JUST BANKS THAT ROB US...

Sometimes miscellaneous costs do the most damage to our wallets, but we never know it. A few extra dollars here and there, and we don't notice. In fact, it's sometimes easier to pay more attention to the big expenses: credit-card bills or student loan payments. But you need to keep an eye on the miscellaneous purchases that can wipe out a fresh $20 faster than you can say Jesse James.

If you've been sticking to a budget, chances are you won't waste a lot of money. Still, there are ceaseless opportunities to save if you keep your eyes open and use a little creativity.

Here are a few methods for making sure that you hold on to as much of your cash so you can use it on better things, like paying your personal retirement fund, saving for long-term goals, or having enough for modest splurges.

A COMPLETE WASTE OF TIME

The 3 Worst Things to Do When Dealing with ATMs:

1. Always go to ATMs that do not belong to your bank.

2. Put throw rugs and easy chairs in the ATM lobby to make it cozy.

3. Light votive candles and pray money comes out of the machine.

Getting Money On Your Side

	The Old Way	The Lazy Way
Bounced Check	$17.39 in penalties	You don't write bad checks
Using the ATM	$2.51 in fees for ATMs around town	Use your bank and pay no off-use charges
Check fees	28 cents per check	Your first 29 checks a month are free at your new bank

Chapter four

Yes, You Can Live Without It! Cut-Throat Cuts to Your Credit Card

What would you do with $1,000? Go on vacation? Set the money aside toward an apartment? Deposit it in a college fund? If you're like most Americans, that $1,000 is what you spend each year on credit-card interest and fees alone.

The United States is awash in credit. And no wonder. We're invited to join exclusive circles of Gold Card holders. We receive "premier" customer service in exchange for paying yearly interest rates of up to 25 percent. Think about that. When was the last time you gave a 25 percent tip? Does your money-market, savings, or certificate of deposit pay close to 25 percent?

Of course, you don't pay interest rates or penalty fees if you always pay your full balance on time. But too many of us carry over debt from month to month, even year to year, and our balances explode to dizzying amounts. In fact, the average credit-card balance for consumers who have to file for bankruptcy is $17,500.

CLIMB OUT OF YOUR CREDIT-CARD DEBT AND AVOID DEEPER TROUBLE

First, you need to know what and where the pitfalls are. Do you know how your interest rate is calculated? Is it by previous balance, or is it calculated on an average daily basis? Do you pay an annual membership fee? Are you shelling out precious resources for quasi-cash? (No, it's not Monopoly money. Quasi-cash means using your credit card to wire money transfers, get foreign currency, obtain traveler's checks, pay taxes, or get casino gambling chips and pay off track bets.)

This chapter will cut through the fine print and double-talk so you can easily spot costly traps. After all, you'd never sign a mortgage, a divorce settlement, or a job contract without reading the fine print. So how about doing the same before you accept that "super" credit-card deal sitting out there in your mailbox?

CREDIT VERSUS DEBIT—EVERYTHING YOU MIXED UP AND IN BETWEEN

It's thin. It's plastic. It's about 3 by 2 $^1/_2$ inches. It must be a credit card. No, it's a debit card. Do you know the differences?

Using the card should be like going on a date; at the very minimum, you need to know its name, its liabilities, and its attributes.

Name: Debit Card

Origin: Debit cards are distributed by your bank where you have a savings or checking account.

Why you use it: A debit card allows you to withdraw money from automated teller machines. You can also use it to charge purchases against your bank account if you don't have cash on hand.

Benefits: Because transactions are instantly subtracted from your account, you can't overspend.

Liabilities:

1. You can be financially liable for unlimited spending if your debit card is stolen, depending on when you report it missing.

   ▪ If you report a stolen card within two days, you can be liable for up to $50.

   ▪ If you notify the card is gone within 60 days, you're liable for up to $500.

   ▪ If you fail to notify the bank that the card was stolen after 60 days, you're liable for an unlimited amount of money.

2. You have no charge-back rights if you get something and want to return it for credit.

3. If you don't record your debit card purchases or withdrawals from your checkbook and keep your balance up to date, you may unknowingly write a bad check.

YOU'LL THANK YOURSELF LATER

Time to shop for holiday or birthday gifts? Leave the credit card at home and use your bank debit card. Each time you make a purchase, the amount will be automatically deducted from your account. You'll spend what you have instead of putting yourself in debt.

Name: Credit Card

Origin: Banks, airlines, and even telephone companies are awarding them to the tune of 30 offers per year (on the average) for each American household. Why you use it: To pay for emergencies, business dinners, anything your heart desires.

Benefits:

1. Emotional/material gratification when you buy what you want. (This is also a liability, as we'll see.)

2. Charge-back rights. You can often get full refunds for merchandise that you return if it was purchased with a credit card.

3. Some cards award benefits like meal discounts or frequent-flyer miles depending on how much you spend.

4. Convenient piece of personal identification.

Liabilities:

1. If it's stolen, you're liable for up to $50.

2. Uncontrolled spending can lead to severe debt. See below for grisly details.

DIRTY LITTLE SECRETS YOU NEED TO KNOW ABOUT CREDIT CARDS

Buyer beware.

You heed that advice when you buy a car, a home, or other goods. Well, you need to beware of how you're paying for that merchandise, too.

Here are some things about your credit card that probably got hidden in the fine print.

Low Monthly Payments Cost You More

You receive an offer in the mail that you "only have to pay 3 percent monthly balance." Sounds great, right?

Wrong! Interest and finance payments are based on what you owe. If you owe more, you will pay more. The less you pay, the faster your interest and other payments will increase because your balance is still large.

New and Interesting Ways Banks Inflate Interest Charges

Day of Purchase versus Day of Posting: Some banks charge interest for items you charge on the day you purchased those goods. That means you're getting charged even before credit-card lenders have even paid a single cent on your behalf.

As a result, your interest payment, which increases over time, will be artificially inflated. To avoid getting stuck, find another card issuer and always pay your balance in full!

Previous Balance: AKA "Raw Deal" or "The Two-Month Swindle"

This is the most common method banks use to calculate the interest you'll pay, and it's absolutely unfair from a consumer's point of view.

Interest is based on your balance from the start of the *last* billing cycle, the so-called "previous balance." In other words, you owe interest for charges you have already "paid off." Confused? Follow closely.

You now know the difference between a debit and credit card. It's not exactly like passing the bar and becoming a lawyer, but go ahead and celebrate your new smarts. Throw a mini graduation party. Hum "Pomp and Circumstance." Raise a toast to yourself. Celebrate!

The Lazy Way

You owe $200 in charges on May 1 (billing cycle no. 1). You pay $100 of that balance by the end of the cycle. You owe $100.

You charge $300 on June 1 (day one of billing cycle no. 2).

Your unpaid charged purchases total $400 ($200 minus $100 plus $300). But you pay interest for $500 worth of charges ($200 balance from May 1, the start of your previous billing cycle, plus $300 for June 1).

Now let's say you pay 1.5 percent interest a month (for an annual 18 percent interest rate). If interest were calculated for the $400 you actually owed, you would pay $6. But interest is based on $500, so you have to shell out $7.50.

You can avoid this inflated interest if your balance is always zero, and you pay your full balance on time, every time.

Average (As in "Not-So-Great-Not-So-Awful") Daily Balance

The interest you pay is based on the average amount you owe in a single billing cycle (20 to 25 days for most banks).

Let's say you owe $200 on May 1. You pay $100 on May 15 (same billing cycle). The average balance for the cycle would be $150, and you would pay interest on that amount. If your bank charges a 1.5 percent interest rate for the month, that means you'll owe $2.25 in interest.

Adjusted (In-Your-Favor) Balance

This is the least commonly used method, which is unfortunate because it is the fairest to the consumer. Interest is calculated by banks after all your payments are deducted from your bill. If you owe $200 on May 1 and pay $100 on May 15 (within the billing cycle), you'll get charged interest for $100 that you still owe. If your bank charges a 1.5 percent interest rate for the month, that means you'll owe $1.50 in interest. If you're lucky enough to find a card that uses this method, go for it!

Penalty Interest Rates

What would you do if a bank offered you a card with a low interest rate but failed to tell you that if you blow it, the rate permanently jumps to a higher rate? And what if "blowing it" meant paying your bill late, exceeding your credit limit (the total amount you can charge), or bouncing a payment check?

Chances are, the original low offer would seem like a risk. Well, banks do penalize bad customers for these reasons, and rates often get hiked by as much as 10 percentage points!

Read the box labeled "Annual Percentage Rate" in your credit-card disclosure to find out how your interest rate is calculated. There should be information there informing you how and why rates will be increased.

Taking from You to Pay Themselves

Be careful if you deposit money at a bank where you got your credit card. You may have signed an agreement when you opened the deposit account (savings, checking) giving your bank the right to take your money to pay delinquent credit-card bills.

YOU'LL THANK YOURSELF LATER

Can't figure out how your interest is calculated on your credit card? Call the card issuer and ask. Better yet, avoid interest by paying off your balances in full and on time.

Charging You Fees Without Telling You They Can Be Waived

You may be paying your credit-card issuers as much as $50 for an annual "membership" fee. If you're a good customer, chances are your credit-card issuer will want to keep you. So ask them to drop the fee to keep you from switching to another card issuer. If you're not a good customer, your request may be denied. Try switching to another card without membership fees or start paying balances on time and try again to get the fee dropped.

Finance Charges for Stuff You've Paid For

Finance charges are just another gimmick banks/issuers employ to make money off of you. (See "Deciphering the Hieroglyphics of Credit-Card Come-Ons" for how finance charges are calculated.) But remember that finance charges accrue until your payment is posted to your account. Pay your bill as soon as possible to keep fees from growing, and be aware that the more your unpaid balance grows, the faster the finance fees increase because they're based as a percentage of your total debt.

Psst. Why That Nifty Grace Period Doesn't Apply to You

Banks have a "grace" period to pay your bill *in full* to pay off your debt, but increasingly, banks are shortening grace periods to 20 days.

If you have outstanding balances, you'll pay finance charges on goods, items, and services, even if you charged them within the current grace period. In other words, grace periods are not a window of opportunity to

QUICK ▥ PAINLESS

That low teaser rate won't last forever. If you can't keep your balance at zero, take note when the low rate expires and higher rates kick in. Mark that date on your calendar, and switch or "hop" to another card with lower rates.

"pay something." You must pay the full amount to get grace.

Wiring In Your Payment May Cost You a Late Fee

Some banks charge late fees. If you mail a bill in long before it's due, you won't get hit with hefty fees that can easily cost more than $20. Banks are not allowed to hold on to your check. They must cash your payment immediately if it is mailed according to their specifications (in the envelope, with stub, and so on, that they require). If you wire in a payment, banks can delay posting the account.

Need a Loan? Need Traveler's Checks? It's Going to Cost You

If you're using your credit card to get cash, you won't just have to pay back the money you borrow. You may have to pay a transaction fee, finance charges, and interest. Interest is calculated from the day you get your cash (so don't get it 10 days before you need it), and it means you'll pay interest even if you pay for your cash advance in full within the same billing cycle!

Transaction fees can be up to 3 percent of the total cash advance you get and usually cap out at $25, and they also apply even if you pay off your cash advance in full and on time.

Cash advances are bad deals, and most financial experts advise that they should be avoided like the bubonic plague.

YOU'LL THANK YOURSELF LATER

Avoid late payments by reminding yourself to send in your credit card payment at least seven to ten days before it's due. Put a reminder on your calendar, your bathroom mirror— anywhere that you'll be sure to get yourself to send in what you owe before you're penalized with late fees.

Remember That $100 You Sent to Pay Your Credit Card Bill? It Didn't All Go to Paying Your Bill

Let's say you owe $500 plus interest and penalty fees. You send in a check for $400. It would be nice to think your balance is now $100. Nice, but probably not realistic.

Banks often don't apply your full payment to your balance (principle). They use some toward interest and fees. This keeps your amount due high, and in turn, lets banks use that inflated number as they continue to calculate interest and other fees.

What it means to you is that the $500 is going to actually cost a lot more by the time you finish paying your bills. Again, pay your new balances in full and on time.

DECIPHERING THE HIEROGLYPHICS OF CREDIT-CARD COME-ONS

So you're beginning to think twice about your credit card. That friendly piece of plastic is deadlier than you thought. But how do you know if you're getting a raw deal or a great one?

Deciphering credit-card agreements can be tough. The print's about as tiny as an ant egg. Unless you have the eyesight of a bat, it's tough getting through the fine print. And it brings new meaning to the word *boring*!

You suspect the guy who wrote your credit-card agreement failed English. Those run-on sentences! How about an adjective to color that pallid prose? Is it any wonder you see 7.9 percent interest on the credit-card offer and just say yes without reading anything else?

Hold on. It's time to look at the fine print. It won't take long if you know what to look for. And by the time you understand what they're really offering you, chances are you won't be bored. You'll be furious.

Get a credit-card offer and pull out the piece of paper that probably is labeled "disclosure" or "agreement." Here we go.

Buzz Words: *credit report*, *different card benefits*, *amendment*

Credit Report

Look for the phrase "credit report." If you see it, you probably are being asked to give the bank the right to look at your personal credit report. Does that matter?

Ask yourself this. Do you want a bank or other issuer to know how many credit cards you have, how much money you have, the name of your employer, where you live, your social security number, the name of your spouse, and whether or not you've lost any lawsuits for monetary damages? All that and more are in your report. (For more details about information in your credit report or how to get your hands on yours, see Chapter 1.)

Different Card Benefits

See that phrase? Chances are it's nestled in a quick fly-by-night sentence somewhere in the introduction that goes something along the lines of: "If we agree that I do not qualify for the Platinum-King-of-The-Universe-Card, you can mail me the Lesser-For-Mortals-Card, which may have different benefits." In other words. All that groovy stuff they offer you may not apply.

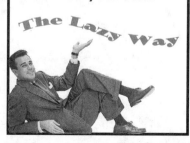

Are you too lazy or tired or apathetic to read your credit card agreement to find out what you really owe? Go over your deal with a friend. Compare what you pay to what he or she pays. Who's getting the better deal? Slogging through the fine print with a friend will help you avoid costly pitfalls, and it will be more fun than figuring out what the fine print really means on your own.

The Lazy Way

QUICK • PAINLESS

Repeat often and make the family say it, too: "If it's charged, it's not free. If it's charged, I must pay. I must pay. I must pay."

Amendments—Not Only in the Bill of Rights!

Banks have the right to "amend" or change the terms of your agreement. Like that reassuring fixed interest? Guess what. They can amend it to a variable rate. Finance rates can be changed. Look for "amendments" throughout the agreement and see what banks can unilaterally change.

Pre-Approved Status

You were so thrilled someone offered you a credit card. After all, it was a surprise. You're so badly in debt, your own mother recently gave you a tin cup and told you to go beg somewhere else. Mom may be tough, but the banks aren't any more nurturing. When they tell you you've been pre-approved, it's just sweet nothing whispered in your ear. Banks can change their minds and not give you that "guaranteed card." Call it the jilted-bride-at-the-altar phenomenon.

The Box

Most credit-card solicitations have a box. On the left are things like annual percentage rate, variable interest rate, grace period. On the right are terms for things like:

- Annual Percentage Rate—This is where you find out how your interest rate will be calculated. This is vital information. You may be astonished to find that your initial credit-card interest rate increases after a certain amount of time. Or you may find you'll get charged a permanently high rate if you pay your balance late or if your check bounces.

- Variable/Fixed Rate—The issuer is telling you your interest can change or stay the same. Remember, banks reserve the right to change the terms, and rates can change even if they are fixed.

- Grace Period—This is where you find out how many days you get to pay your *full* balance before you have to pay finance charges. If you don't pay your balance in full and on time, the grace period does not apply, even for new purchases.

- Annual Membership Fee—These can range as high as $50 a year, or it may be zero. Competition is so fierce for good credit-card customers that you often may be able to call up and ask to get it waived.

Minimum Finance Charge (and Why It Only Grows and Grows)

Look at the credit-card agreement under a paragraph that probably is labeled something obvious like *finance charges*. This is where you find out how the bank calculates the charge.

In general, banks use your Annual Percentage Rate to calculate finance charges. They divide the APR by 365 (the number of days in a year) to get what they call a Daily Periodic Rate. That daily rate may seem small to you, but hold on! The finance fee accrues each day a balance goes unpaid. If your debt grows, your finance charge will get bigger, too.

Late Payment Fee

Fees can run as high as $25 and possibly more if you don't pay your bill on time. Don't wait until the last minute to

pay your bill, or you may blow through your deadline. If you think you might mail your check too late, it might be cheaper to spend a little extra to express or overnight mail your payment to your issuer rather than paying a $25 overdue fee.

Fee for Exceeding Credit Line

Charges can also be as high as $25. Is it really worth it asking to charge more, especially if you're already in debt? (Please note, there's only one correct answer to this question, and it begins with an *N*!)

HOW TO BEAT CREDIT-CARD ISSUERS AT THEIR OWN GAME AND AVOID TROUBLE

1. It can't be said enough. Pay in full. Pay on time.

2. Keep no more than one or two credit cards.

3. Do not carry your cards with you. If you don't have them, you can't use them.

4. Each time you use the card, subtract the amount you charge from your checkbook or, if you have no checkbook, from your savings. If you bounce a check or clear out your nest egg getting a certain item, then you shouldn't be using the credit card.

5. Put a Post-It® on your card and record the total amount of each credit-card transaction when you use it to keep track of how much you're spending.

7. Hop, Skip, Jump. If you're paying off a card that has a high interest rate, try transferring it to a card with

a lower rate. But remember to change cards again before the rate goes up!

8. Don't use the card for cash advances.

If you're trying to reduce your debt, pay the card that costs you the most money in fees, penalties, and interest. If you want to consolidate, consider paying all the bills with a loan from a bank or credit union, which most certainly will charge you lower interest. Then pay the credit union or bank on time.

Warning! Do not take out any loans to pay credit-card debts if you have even the slightest suspicion that you can't control your credit-card spending. You can't borrow your way out of debt, because you'll end up getting into deeper financial trouble.

WHERE TO GET THE BEST DEALS IN CREDIT CARDS

Don't just ask your buddy who works for Visa. There are a zillion places that rate credit cards, and many are on the Internet, so you can get free information. But here are a few good places to start:

Bank Rate Monitor
11811 U.S. Highway 1
North Palm Beach, FL 33408
(561) 627-7330
www.bankrate.com

Bank Rate supplies consumers with information on credit cards, mortgage rates, auto loans, and ATM fees.

Call your state banking department or Department of Consumer Affairs to find out if those agencies can mail you a free comparison of credit-card rates, fees, and

A COMPLETE WASTE OF TIME

The 3 Worst Things to Do When Paying Off Credit Cards:

1. Consolidate your credit-card debts as you pay them off.

2. Always pay off the card with the lowest interest rates first and save the really expensive bills for last.

3. Keep a wide collection of credit cards so you have choices when it's time to charge those purchases.

You've been careful about choosing your credit card. You know you're paying the lowest interest. You have no yearly fees, and you have a long grace period to pay off your balances. Reward yourself for tracking down such a great deal. Buy yourself a small gift or take yourself out to a fun outing—but use cash to pay for your treat!

The Lazy Way

grace periods. Remember, the phone number for state agencies may be toll-free, so call (800) 555-1212 to see if you can get a free number in your area.

Other Must-Contact Resources

Consumer World
www.consumerworld.org

Consumer World is an electronic yellow pages of websites having to do with credit cards, debt, and loans. Founder and consumer attorney, Edgar Dworsky, red flags really great sites, and it is a good place to visit if you're looking for information on a variety of financial, debt, and consumer issues.

National Center for Financial Education
P.O. Box 34070
San Diego, CA 92163
(619) 232-8811

This nonprofit began in 1982, and it can send consumers free educational information about credit cards, investing, saving, and other financial planning methods.

Consumer Federation of America
1424 16th St. NW — Suite 694
Washington, DC 20036
(202) 387-6121

These are the thorn in the credit-card issuers' side. CFA does annual surveys of credit-card debt and keeps track of folks who hand out the cards.

Getting Money on Your Side

	The Old Way	The Lazy Way
Annual Fee	Up to $50 a year	Nothing! Get it waived.
Credit-Card Offer	Banks can increase your payments, hidden in interest and fees	Save $1,000 per year in fees by knowing how to avoid them
Interest	Up to 25 percent/year	Switch to lower rates

Part 3

Home-Cheap-Home with Low-Cost Luxury

Are you too lazy to read Home-Cheap-Home with Low-Cost Luxury?

1 You've had your clunker fixed so many times that the local garage has given you your own special "Buy 10 Mufflers, Get One Free" card. ☐ yes ☐ no

2 Not a good sign. Your father opened the tuition bill, and without a beat said, "Son? What son? That's not my kid. This isn't my bill. Young man, I'm afraid you're going to have to find someone else to pay this. Best of luck." ☐ yes ☐ no

3 The bill from your triple bypass surgery sent you back into cardiac arrest. ☐ yes ☐ no

Managing Your Mortgage Without Going Mad

Except for saddle burn and the long trip to the grocery store, it must have been great getting a home in the wild west. All you had to do was stake a claim, herd some cattle, and work the land. With a little sweat equity, the property was yours. No mortgages. No rental deposit fees. No lawyers.

Your home—be it the picket-fence variety or an urban studio—is probably your biggest expense. Rent and mortgage payments are unavoidable costs that sometimes leave little to pay the bills or buy anything else. Still, there are ways to save on mortgage payments, and if you're a renter, your landlord may be legally obligated to make some repairs to that over-priced room you call home.

The first thing you need to do before you choose a home or a mortgage is get a copy of your credit report. If you have a poor rating, you'll end up paying more in interest. There are three major credit-reporting agencies where you can obtain your report. Equifax (800) 685-1111; Experian (800) 682-7654; or Trans Union (800) 916-8800. (To find out how to do a credit check, refer to chapter 1.)

MONEY-SAVING MORTGAGE MECHANISMS

Does your dream home have a sprawling garden? Is it nestled among acres of midwestern corn fields? Is it an apartment overlooking San Francisco's Golden Gate Bridge? Chances are you've spent a long time thinking about your ideal nest. That's why you probably didn't—or won't—buy the first house or apartment you see. You want to look around. Compare. See what you can get for your money.

It's a pity most of us stop doing our homework after we've picked out the home we're going to buy, when it's time to get a home loan. Too often, people end up spending too much on the wrong kind of agreement for their lifestyles and income. Most first-time home buyers opt for a 30-year fixed variety because they want to stretch out their payments. But long-term mortgages have the highest interest rates, and long-term may not be a good idea for everyone. After all, the average buyer stays in her first home nine years before trading up.

If you're just starting to look for a new place, put at least as much energy into learning about mortgages as you do about your actual home. And if you already have a mortgage, it may not be too late to search for ways to trim your expenses by a little or by hundreds of thousands of dollars. All it takes to save is a little homework.

MORTGAGES DON'T COME FROM THE STORK, AND THEY DON'T GROW ON TREES

Mortgages are most commonly offered by banks and savings and loans. But credit unions and mortgage bankers also lend money for home purchases. Mortgage brokers are middlemen who link the borrower (that's you) with a lender.

All these lenders mean they'll compete for your business. Shop around for the best deals.

1. Find out about the lender.

What type of loans do they offer?

- Fixed (interest rate stays the same)

- Adjustable or variable (interest rate changes)

- Growing Equity Mortgage (interest rate stays the same, but your payment grows over time)

- Graduated Payment Mortgage (interest rate increases over time, which makes it attractive to consumers who believe their own income also will increase)

How long do you want your mortgage to be? 15 years? 30 years? Longer? Shorter? What are their interest rates for different mortgages? How do they compare to other lending institutions? What fees would you pay? Are there other service costs?

You should compare all costs and figures with other lending institutions to give you a sense of where you can get the best deal. Luckily, you don't have to be an

Buying a home is exciting and scary. And looking for mortgage deals can be daunting, too. If you're living, eating, and dreaming about home-loans and interest rates, be sure to take a mental break from it all during this process for a little fun. Look at interior design magazines, walk by homes you like, or draw pictures of how you might want to decorate your new nest after the financial work is done and you have the cash to get your nest.

The Lazy Way

economics professor to get to know the market. The Internet has a few good websites for mortgage ratings. Call local lenders and just ask. Scan newspaper ads, or talk to friends and family to get word-of-mouth referrals for you to investigate. But whatever you do, don't accept the first deal you're offered.

Helpful Resources

Bank Rate Monitor
1811 U.S. Highway 1
North Palm Beach, FL 33408
(561) 627-7330
www.bankrate.com

Bank Rate compares credit card, auto loan, and bank rates nationwide.

Quicken Mortgage
www.quicken.com

Quicken rates both fixed- and variable-rate mortgages. But the site omits names of lenders, so it acts as a mortgage broker.

HSH Associates
1200 Route 23
Butler, NJ
(800) 873-2837
www.hsh.com

Each week, HSH compares over 2,500 mortgage lenders from across the country and publishes the survey in its report, "Updates," which can be mailed or e-mailed

YOU'LL THANK YOURSELF LATER

Don't just go to the bank or savings and loan your real estate agent recommends. Start shopping around for the best mortgage deals before you even look for your dream home. If you have a computer, there are many Internet sites that list quick, free comparisons of rates offered by lenders near you. Scouting for great deals before you buy will save thousands of dollars in mortgage payments.

directly to you. The HSH "Homebuyer's Mortgage Kit" lists mortgage deals from lenders found in a buyer's area, and it publishes an informative and easy-to-understand guide to home financing. The kit costs $23, including postage and handling.

Veribanc

(800) 442-2657 or (800) 837-4226

Veribanc offers phone ratings on banks, savings and loans, and credit union mortgages.

LOVE ME, LOVE MY MORTGAGE

You have your home. You make your payments. Is it too late, or can you save on your mortgage now that you've moved in? (Do you really think we're going to say no?) Here's how:

1. Refinance and join the good times:

Interest rates rise and fall as sure as the sun rises and the moon gets full at least once a month. You don't really need to know why. It could be inflation (rates go up). It could be that the economy needs a shot in the arm (rates go down to spur growth). Or Federal Reserve Chairman Alan Greenspan looks flustered (everyone shudders). What's important is this:

Low interest rates = Cheaper to borrow money.

High interest rates = Expensive to borrow.

When rates are low, as they have been in 1998, it's a great time to consider refinancing. If you have a variable (changing) loan, you might want to lock in on a fixed (steady) rate. Refinancing will cost you money in fees, so

YOU'LL THANK YOURSELF LATER

So you know a bit about what mortgages are going for, what's a great interest rate, and what's a bum steer. But what about you? What are your needs? Ask yourself this:

What can I afford to pay each month?

What type of mortgage best suits my needs?

If I plan to move soon, a long-term, 30-year mortgage may be too expensive. (The longer the mortgage, the more the lender charges in interest.) Will I be able to pay more interest in the future? A Graduated Payment Mortgage might best suit my needs.

Answering these questions will help you get the best deal.

QUICK 🐷 PAINLESS

you need to ask yourself if those fees are worth the savings.

Can you afford to refinance? Will you be in your home long enough to make refinancing worth it? A lender must provide you a good-faith estimate of what the total closing cost will be to refinance, including closing costs, attorney fees, appraisal fees, and other expenses.

2. Biweekly Mortgages—The Path to Saving Thousands

Instead of paying monthly mortgage payments, divide that amount in two and pay biweekly. What's the difference? Paying your mortgage every two weeks is equivalent to 13 monthly payments instead of 12. So a 30-year mortgage paid in biweekly installments takes 23 years to pay off. A 15-year mortgage will be cut down to roughly 12 years. What does this mean in terms of savings? How about hundreds of thousands of dollars.

The table represents Mama and Papa Bear's mortgage payments. Mama and Papa Bear buy their dream home in the woods for $357,000. They're paying a fixed,

	Monthly Payment	Biweekly Payment
Amount Paid	$4,201.97	$2,100.99
Loan cut time	0 years	9 years
Total interest	$537,404.79	$343,950
SAVINGS	None	$193,453.86

7.75 percent interest rate for 30 years. After living there for two years, they start thinking about making biweekly payments so they can set some money aside for baby bear's college fund. Here's what they save, according to one mortgage company:

Variation on a Theme: Biweekly Payment Part II

Don't have the cash flow to make payments every two weeks? Figure out what a monthly payment would be ($4,201.97 if we're using the Bears as an example). Divide that by 12 (for months). That's $350.15.

Pay that amount every month, and it will add up to that extra, 13th payment per year. You'll save just as much time and money as if you had made biweekly payments.

NOTE: Mortgage experts say it is vital to clearly indicate that extra payments be dedicated toward the principle of your loan, not to interest. Mail the extra money in a separate envelope with a letter clearly indicating you want the money to go toward your debt.

RENTERS' RIGHTS

Pity the poor serf. He toiled and toiled from sun up until sun down. And for what? Cramped lodging with a leaky roof, no central heating, and a cold, dirt floor. When you think about your place, it's clear not much has changed since the Middle Ages. You work hard for your own leaky roof, while your landlord lives in a sprawling country spread, made possible by your rent.

Take a page from history. The serfs had their rebellions. You have your rights. There are bills and services

A COMPLETE WASTE OF TIME

The 3 Worst Things to Do When Trying to Save Money:

1. Pay mortgage managers hundreds of dollars a year to get you to pay your mortgage twice a month. (Yes, there really are people who do this!) Why should you keep the money for yourself?

2. Avoid biweekly payments. Stick with the monthly ones.

3. Pay your roommate to wash your dishes.

Before you move into your new rental, go through your nest with the landlord and make a list of holes, scratches, and other items to be fixed. Take photos of the apartment, too. When you move out you won't get stuck paying for damages you didn't cause and get that landlord to repair items before you move in.

your landlord has to pay. And let's face it, if you're renting, you need all the help you can get. The more expenses you can avoid, the more you can save for your own place one day.

■ **Is it worn out and torn out, or did you break it?**

Are the walls of your new apartment covered in marks? Or are the stains on the wall evidence from your last food fight? If ordinary wear and tear has caused problems—worn rugs, broken dishwasher, leaky plumbing—then it's up to your landlord to make necessary repairs. But if you've ruined the walls with food, poured paint on the hardwood floor, and washed heavy equipment in your dishwasher, and caused any other damage, then it's up to you to fix everything.

■ **Did your landlord just spend your security deposit on a steak dinner?**

Your landlord has to refund your security deposit, and she must pay you the interest that deposit earns while it is safely kept at a bank. You may lose the money if you move out before your lease expires.

■ **Can you sublet or break your lease early?**

Many landlords will refund your security deposit if you find a tenant to take your place. A sublet can help you keep that nifty home if you have to move out of town for a few months. Try to make sure your lease agreement allows you to sublet and what the consequences will be if you move out early.

■ **Be safe and secure.**

Your landlord has to make sure you're safe. If there's no lock on the door, it's up to him to get one. If the apartment needs child-safety bars on the windows, you have a right to demand them.

Take a Picture, Capture the Moment, and Protect Your Pocketbook

- Before you move into your new digs, take pictures of the place. If there's a crack in the bathroom tiles, you'll have evidence that you didn't break it and shouldn't have to pay to replace it. Your landlord has to refund your deposit when you leave, but he or she can keep money to replace or restore any property damage you caused. If you have the pictures, you'll be sure to get all your money back.

- Read your lease agreement! You don't want to find out that your pet iguana can't move in with you after you've just signed a year's lease.

- Consider buying renter's insurance. Renter's insurance costs about $300 to $400 a year and will protect you from theft, natural disasters, or damages that someone else causes.

- Pay your rent on time. If you default on rent, it can hurt your credit report. You might not care today, but when it comes time to borrow money for a home, a bad credit rating could stop you from getting a loan. Of course, withholding rent while you settle a dispute with your landlord is another matter

A COMPLETE WASTE OF TIME

The 3 Worst Things to Do When Renting:

1. Sign a rental agreement without reading (and understanding!) the document.

2. Pay a deposit without getting a receipt.

3. Get a rental agreement that does not allow you to sublease your place if you need to move out for some time. You may end up paying for two rents if you can't have your baby brother move in while you're in Bora Bora.

entirely. Make sure that you're legally allowed to withhold payment in your state before you do so, however.

Know the law. Renters' rights vary from state to state. Call the state Department of Consumer Affairs and ask for a copy of state law regarding tenant's rights. There are several books on renter's rights that also may be useful. Check out publications like *Every Tenant's Legal Guide* by lawyers Janet Portman and Marcia Stewart (published by Nolo Press). Or call HUD to find out what federal laws protect you.

HUD
451 Seventh St. SW, Suite 5100
Washington, DC 20410
(800) 669-9777

Getting Money on Your Side

	The Old Way	The Lazy Way
30-year mortgage	30 years of monthly payments and no savings in interest	23 years of biweekly payments and $100,000 saved in interest
New stair banister	$100 for you	Nothing. Your landlord has to pay.
Mortgage manager	Up to $500/year	Nothing. Manage your own payments.

Flip the Switch: Easy Ways to Cut Energy Costs

Ernest Hemingway wrote that everyone needs a clean, well lighted place, and you agree. You keep the lights on so that when you return home from work, the apartment isn't dark and dreary. And you just love those winter beach parties. (Jack up the thermostat to 92 degrees, play old Beach Boys tapes, and drink fruity rum drinks. Voila! Daytona Beach in Detroit.) The trouble is, your utility bills are horrendous.

It seems you're not the only one burning money. Every year, the average American family spends roughly $1,300 on utility bills, and most of that money is wasted on unnecessary energy, according the U.S. Department of Energy.

Here's the good news. There are dozens and dozens of ways to stop spending so much. Of course, starting with the basics—like turning off lights when you leave a room—is an obvious place to start saving. But how about knowing once

Heating and cooling your home eats up more energy (and dollars) than other uses. Air conditioners also can drive up bills in the summertime, so it's often better to spend more today for an energy-efficient unit. Air conditioners are measured by their SEER (Seasonal Energy Efficiency Ratio). Think of it as miles-per-gallon on a car. The Department of Energy says anything that has a 12 to 16 SEER ratio is efficient. (The higher the number, the more efficient the air conditioner will be.) The average SEER for air conditioners sold in the U.S. is roughly 10 SEER, so shop around!

Source: U.S. Department of Energy

and for all which drives up your water bills the most: running a dishwasher or washing dishes by hand? (I'll tell you later.)

If you know what uses up the most energy, the most watts, and the most water, then you'll be surprised by how many ways you can find to cut back. And here's the best news of all: Simple cost-cutting techniques can shave off 10 to 50 percent of your bill. That's $130 to $650 a year!

You can even trim costs when you trim the lawn yourself. And speaking of cutting the grass, let's talk about self-reliance. Contractors, electricians, and plumbers all cost money. Isn't it time you learned how to do some basic fix-its around the place instead of paying someone $60 an hour to hammer a nail into your wall? Besides, you'd probably look pretty cute in a tool belt.

HOW ENERGY-SAVVY ARE YOU?

You suspect that your refrigerator eats up a lot of energy. But how about the guppy aquarium? Or the television? Know your appliances, and then you can start targeting where you're going to save. The more energy you use, or the higher the wattage on things like light-bulbs (above 60 watts is high), the faster you use up energy, and the higher your utility bills will be.

Waste Not, Watt Not—Ways to Save
The Kitchen

1. Cook as many meals at one time as you can either in the oven or on top of your range. If meals need

different temperatures—200 degrees, 250 degrees, and 300 degrees—use the average temperature (250 degrees). This will save energy. Moreover, cooking in bulk will save you time if you can freeze some of the food and eat it later, or take it to lunch instead of eating out. That will help you cut costs, too!

2. Turn off the oven or range just before you're done cooking. The heat will finish the job.

3. Stop peeking at the cookies! Every time you open the oven door, the temperature drops 25 degrees. Inefficient!

4. Don't use little pots on big ranges. The extra surface on the range wastes energy. (Call it the Goldie-Locks-in-Pappa-Bear-Chair phenomenon.)

QUICK ⬛ PAINLESS

A watched pot may not boil, but an uncovered one takes its time to cook, too. When you're cooking, cover the pot. It will reduce the amount of time it takes for food to heat or for water to come to a boil. That saves you cooking time and cuts the energy needed to run your gas or electric range.

Energy User	Daily Use	Kilowatts per year (1 Kilowatt = 1,000 watts)
Aquarium	All the time	700 kilowatts
Water heater (40 gallon)	2 hours a day	2,190 kilowatts
Microwave oven	2 hours a week	89 kilowatts
Refrigerator	All the time	642 kilowatts
Color television	4 hours a day	292 kilowatts (read books!)
Vacuum	1 hour a week	38 kilowatts
Hair dryer	15 min. a day	100 kilowatts

The Lazy Way

5. Run a full dishwasher. It uses less water (about 6 gallons) than washing those dishes by hand (20 gallons).

6. Air-dry your dishes instead of using the heat drying cycle on the dishwasher.

7. Why root around for the milk every single morning and leave the fridge door open? Put popular items up front and keep the cool air in.

8. To make your refrigerator as efficient as possible, let air circulate around the food in the main compartment, but fill in empty space in the freezer. (If you don't have frozen food, use bags of ice to fill in the empty spaces.)

9. Going on an extended vacation? Consider cleaning out and unplugging the fridge (and the lights, TV, radio, and water heater).

10. Refrigerators with a freezer on top are more energy efficient than freezers on the side.

11. Defrost your fridge and freezer! Frost buildup increases the amount of energy needed to keep the motor running. (Besides, isn't it time you got brave and looked at what's in that frozen Tupperware™?)

12. Good doors make good utility bills. Make sure your refrigerator and freezer doors are airtight. Test them by closing the door on a piece of paper (or your last dollar). If you can pull the paper easily, the door seal is too loose, and cool air is escaping.

13. Cover those leftovers. Uncovered food not only smells like a high-school chemistry experiment, it also increases the moisture in the refrigerator, so more energy is used to keep the motor running.

14. Clean out refrigerator coils at least once a year. It will prolong the life of the machine.

15. Don't set the temperature too low on the fridge or freezer. A refrigerator should be set at 37 degrees to 40 degrees Fahrenheit. The freezer should be zero to five degrees. You want colder? Go to the South Pole.

The Bathroom

1. Four words: Low-flow shower head.

2. Don't waste water. Turn off the tap when you're just standing there gazing at your reflection in the mirror.

3. Keep a plunger in the bathroom. You'd be amazed how much you can plunge out of the pipes without having to spend your life's savings on a plumber.

The Laundry Room

1. Most energy used on washing machines—up to 85 percent—is used to heat water. Use less water or cool water when you do your wash to trim energy costs.

2. Front-loaded washers use about a third of the energy and less water than top-loading machines, so you spend less on electric and water bills.

IF YOU'RE SO
INCLINED

The federal government requires that appliances must be affixed with bright-yellow and black "Energy Guide" labels. The stickers tell you how much energy an appliance uses. Compare labels among certain kinds of appliances to find the most efficient model. The extra effort will keep your utility bills from exploding.

When you shop for a new appliance, look for something called the Energy Star label. The label means that the U.S. Departments of Energy and Environmental Protection found that the appliance exceeds federal standards. In other words, getting an appliance with this label can save you a bundle in the long run.

A new refrigerator with an Energy Star label should save you up to $70 a year compared with that old clunker you bought 15 years go, according to the Department of Energy. That means savings can top $1,000 during the average 15-year lifetime of a refrigerator.

3. Don't put two socks and a pair of shorts in a big load. It's a waste of water and energy.

4. Get that old-fashioned, summer smell. Dry your clothes outside.

Entertainment Centers

1. Turn off the radio and TV when you're not using them.

2. Turn down the volume to reduce the amount of wattage needed to run the radio.

3. Remember these? Books.

Phone

1. Only make long-distance calls when the rates are low (usually nights or weekends).

2. Go epistolary. Write a letter.

3. Use e-mail instead of long-distance calls. (Write letters offline, and then log on to send them.)

4. Put an egg timer by the phone when you make long distance calls to keep from talking too long.

5. Keep a notebook by the phone and record calls and length of conversation to keep track of how often you're using it. If it's too much work to track all of your gossip, keep a list of long-distance calls.

6. Always ask if a company has a toll-free number and use that.

7. Ditch the cellular phone and enjoy some peace and quiet. Or give out your number to your boss and

your mother. Your friends can reach you when you get home, and you won't pay for those calls.

8. Use a phone book. Dialing 411 for information or *69 to find out who just called and hung up on you can cost you roughly 75 cents each time. Those "conveniences" add up.

GENERAL HOUSEHOLD COST-CUTTING TIPS

Lighting:

1. Turn off the lights when you aren't using them!

2. Use an automatic timer to turn lights on or off when you're not home.

3. Replace bulbs with lower wattage.

4. Less is more. A 100-watt incandescent bulb makes more light than three 40-watt bulbs but uses 20 watts less than electricity. In short, use one large bulb instead of lots of small-watt bulbs.

5. If you can use three-way bulbs, switch to lower watts when you don't need as much light.

6. Candles. Look what they did for Abe Lincoln and Romeo.

7. Dimmers can help save energy by cutting the lighting level, and by extension, cutting wattage. Dimmers are easy to install, but make sure you turn off the fuse box or circuit breaker. Use a circuit tester to ensure that the power is off, or you're in for quite a nasty shock! (If you think "fuse box" is

QUICK ⬤ PAINLESS

Instead of paying an electric bill to keep the television going, why not try for some live entertainment? Take turns reading a gripping mystery out loud. Read a chapter a night, just like an ongoing miniseries. Or read to yourself—stand up and emote! These pastimes are free, and better yet, no commercials!

YOU'LL THANK YOURSELF LATER

Take out the incandescent bulbs in your lights and replace them with energy-efficient fluorescent bulbs. They cost more than incandescent bulbs, but they last up to 10 times longer, so they'll save you money in the long run.

- Replace 40-watt incandescent with 11-watt compact fluorescent

- Replace 60-watt incandescent with 15-watt compact fluorescent

- Replace 75-watt incandescent with 18-watt compact fluorescent

- Replace 100-watt incandescent with 27-watt compact fluorescent

the name of a hot, techno-pop group, you probably should hire an electrician to do the job.)

Heating and Cooling:

1. Keep air conditioner filters clean. Dirty filters restrict air flow and make the air conditioner less efficient.

2. The temperature controls in your home or apartment should not be lower than 78 degrees in the summer or higher than 68 degrees in the winter.

3. Wear a sweater instead of turning up the thermostat.

4. Use storm windows to keep your home warm in the winter.

5. Put weather stripping around windows and doors to keep drafts from blowing under your door. Weather stripping comes in easy-to-use adhesive rolls, so even if you don't know the difference between a hammer and a wrench, you can do the job!

6. Tired of that cold, lonely bed? Use grandma's old quilt or extra blankets to stay warm and comfy instead of an electric blanket. Feet cold? Wear socks to bed until you warm up.

7. Be artistic! Draw the drapes, and then close them, too. It will keep your apartment cooler in the day.

8. Try a window fan before you use an air conditioner. It will be less expensive to operate.

9. If you go away on vacation, turn off the hot water heater and set the water heater to 120-degrees.

THE GARDEN

Forget sin, shame, and the embarrassment of being bamboozled by a reptile. The real reason Adam and Eve started crying when they were booted from the Garden of Eden is because they dreaded their utility bills.

Plants are an amazing way to save on cooling and heating expenses. The Department of Energy estimates they can cut costs by as much as 25 percent. Deciduous trees (the ones that lose their leaves) do the best job at cutting heat whey they are placed around the house. The folks at Lawrence Berkeley National Laboratory in northern California, where they hug trees because of the heat, estimate that daytime temperatures in the summer can be cut by as much as 6 degrees in tree-shaded neighborhoods. In the winter, bare leaves let sunlight reach and warm your home. Vines also provide shade.

Don't forget evergreen trees (the ones that stay green year-round). They deflect winter winds if you plant them on the north side of your house.

Energy-Saving Resources

U.S. Department of Energy
Energy Efficiency and Renewable Energy Clearinghouse
P.O. Box 3048
Merrifield, VA 22116
(800) DOE-EREC
http://doe.erec@nciinc.com

This is where the government's best energy gurus meet. They can answer any questions you may have, tell your kid to listen to you and turn off the light, or furnish

QUICK ◑ PAINLESS

Go to the local creek, dive into your neighbor's swimming pool, or check out the city recreation pool. A midday dip will cool you down better than an air conditioner, and it's a lot more fun than sitting inside all day.

you with information about the appliances that drive up your utility bill.

There is also a lot of free information you can use! Look on the last bill from your electric or gas company, and there should be a phone number for questions or comments. If you can't find one, then call any number you see. Ask them if they have any materials on how you can reduce your bill. Most will happily send you information. Even in New York City, where everything is for sale, Con Edison provides customers who ask with a free, informative (and well-written) booklet called "How to Cut Energy Costs in Your Apartment."

TANTALIZING TOOLBOX TIPS THAT SAVE A BUNDLE

We all have those fantasies. For women, it's the "Thelma and Louise" vision (sans cliff). Strong, feisty women who laugh when the drain pipe under their kitchen sink clogs with a nasty snarl. Plumber? Bah! They've got an auger, a snake cable, and they're good to go. For guys, it's not having to ask a plumber to fix the dishwasher.

Being capable is also cost effective. And everyone, from a baron of an ivy-covered country estate to struggling writers in an unheated loft, should be able to make minor repairs.

Too intimidated to try? Think about this. Would you rather pay a guy named Ed $60 an hour to tighten a bolt, or would you rather have the money to pay your bills, buy yourself a treat, or save for a rainy day. You've got nothing to lose but money if you don't try.

Feeling chilly? Cuddle with your true love. (If you have a large, slobbery dog or a friendly cat, they'll do, too.)

The Lazy Way

First things first. You need a tool kit. If you have the basics, you can run out and get the perfect sized nail. But if you don't have a hammer or other basics, you're stuck.

Must-Have Tools:

- Hammer
- Screwdriver: flat-head and Phillips
- 6-inch and 8-inch adjustable wrench
- Vice grips
- Allen wrench
- Pliers
- Tape measure (make sure it's longer than a foot)
- Flashlight (with working batteries!)
- Staple gun
- Hand saw

Optional Tools:

- Electric drill with variable speeds
- Drill bits
- Carpenter's level (good for building shelves)
- Black electrical tape
- Extension cord (the one on the drill is pretty short)

Other Good Stuff:

- Paint brushes
- Paint thinner
- Drop cloth
- Jar filled with small nails for quick jobs like hanging pictures or coat racks

A COMPLETE WASTE OF TIME

The 3 Worst Things to Do When Saving Money in the Summer:

1. Water your plants in the middle of a hot day. Much of the water you pay for is just evaporating.

2. Cover yourself with a fig leaf, stand in the sprinkler, and ask your neighbors to throw money at you like a human wishing well to earn extra cash. You'll drive up your water bill and probably end up getting arrested.

3. Dig a hole in the yard, fill it with water, and invite your friends to roll in the mud and "relive Woodstock." Who cares if you have to pay for the water, repair the lawn, and explain your behavior to your wife.

IF YOU'RE SO
INCLINED

Are you in a low-income bracket? (Honey, aren't we all?) Seriously, if you're really broke, you may qualify for a free home weatherization program that's funded by the U.S. Department of Energy's Efficiency Clearinghouse (address on p. 77). Contact the agency for more information. There's no harm in asking for free help to cut those bills!

- Carpenter's glue
- Circuit tester

Resources:

www.housenet.com

This website has a wealth of free information on home improvement, home repairs, gardening tips, decorating, and even a "project of the month." It's a great way to learn how to do basic chores that might otherwise cost you a small fortune.

www.homenet.com

Another great source of information on home improvement, tools, ideas, and tips. There's even a place to ask questions in case you can't remember where that extra bolt came from.

Care for Your Home The Lazy Way

Filled with tips and shortcuts to keep your house in tip-top shape (and repair stuff when things *aren't* so tip-top). Author: Terry Meany.

Getting Money On Your Side

	The Old Way	The Lazy Way
New dimmer switch	$60 an hour to hire an electrician	$2.54 for a new switch if you replace it.
Winter warmth	$200 monthly heating bill	Sweater and quilt —free warmth!
Summer cooling	Air conditioning fees	Plant trees near your home and trim 25 percent from your utility costs.

Fantastic Ways to Finagle Your Food and Grocery Budget, Even If You're Finicky

Man cannot live on bread alone. And in your case, you can't live without the kid who delivers your pizza, the vending machine at the office, and the microwave. You have a feeling that your shopping and dining habits are taking a big bite out of your budget. You start the day with $20 in your wallet, and by night, when you buy your last bag of Doritos, there's nothing left but a couple of forlorn nickels.

We all need to eat, of course. But enjoying a good meal and feeding yourself doesn't have to cost a fortune. That doesn't mean you don't deserve to splurge on a great meal. In fact, it's probably not the once-in-a-blue-moon, three-star dinners that hit you the hardest. It's the small stuff: frozen yogurts, dinners from the drive-through window, convenience

It's early morning. You make coffee, open the refrigerator, and...no milk! It's inconvenient not to have food in the house, and it's also expensive. Keep your kitchen stocked with a variety of "staples" so you always can make yourself a meal and avoid eating out. Good things to have on hand include milk, eggs, butter, cereal, juice, pasta, fruit, and veggies. Freeze poultry or beef and thaw it when you need it.

(microwave or prepared) meals, and cafe lattés from a specialty coffeehouse that may be causing you the most damage.

Consider this. Take-out meals—dinners you get at places like Boston Market—cost Americans roughly $80 billion a year. Keeping track of what you're eating (in dollars and cents) will quickly show you where you can cut back.

Then there's your kitchen. Do you know where it is? Can you tell the difference between a spatula and a whisk? Cooking your own meals also will save your wallet. Nearly half of the roughly $690 billion we spend on food each year goes for meals cooked by other people outside our home, according to NDP Group, which tracks Americans' dining habits.

So, crack and egg or two, throw it in a lightly greased pan, and enjoy your first scrambled egg. It's not hard to do, and you'll be well on your way to cheaper, tastier, and often healthier eating. (For more quick and easy cooking ideas, pick up *Cook Your Meals The Lazy Way.*)

THE VAST ABYSS YOU CALL YOUR STOMACH

How much did you spend today on food? Do you have any idea? The first step to reining in your costs is to track them. Try to do this for a week, but a day will be okay, too, if you don't have the time. Choose a typical day for you in terms of your eating habits. (Don't use the day your boss takes you to lunch and mom and dad buy you dinner.)

Keeping Track of Groceries

Start keeping receipts for groceries and other household items (paper towels, garbage bags, Lysol). Now, take a look at your budget, the one you made after reading Chapter 2 of this book. Are you spending more than you planned? Even if you don't have a budget, look at your receipts. Ask yourself the following:

1. What am I spending?

2. What am I buying? (Do I get a lot of microwave meals? Am I buying staples like dried pasta and ingredients to make my own dinners instead of ordering from "Pasta to Go" every night? Is there a lot of costly junk food?)

3. Did I use coupons?

4. Did I get any generic substitutes for products, or do I buy name-brand only?

5. Did I buy a lot of things at once, or do I go the store every day for last-minute buys?

If you're buying a lot of prepared food, name-brand products, or shopping just before you need to make dinner, then chances are you're wasting quite a bit of money.

Grocery Shopping Debt Busters

If you're buying your food and staples at the 24-hour-a-day corner store, you're shopping at the wrong place. Where you shop has as big an impact on your wallet as what you get. Go to large supermarket chains that have

YOU'LL THANK YOURSELF LATER

Keeping track of what you spend on food may make you hungry. Buy your favorite treat (not caviar or Moet) in bulk. Have some now, and save some for later. You'll save money buying a bigger portion, and you'll stop that awful grumbling in your stomach.

"bonus savers" clubs, wide selections of products, generic items, and sales. Discount warehouses are great, too. And large pharmacies, like CVS and Rite Aid, often can't be beat for inexpensive household supplies.

Once you get to the store, start shopping smart!

1. Shop on a regular schedule, but no more than once a week. If you keep running out for items, you'll probably deviate from your budget.

2. Don't shop when you're hungry! Even the canned sardines and anchovies will begin looking tempting. Impulse buys can cost you more than you planned.

3. Shop with a grocery list. If you count on "remembering" what you need, you'll end up buying impulse items like ice cream and forget staples, like bread and milk.

4. Put a notation next to grocery list items that you have coupons for. This will keep you from forgetting to get a better deal when you get to the checkout counter.

5. Read unit prices. Those are the numbers on the left side of the sales price. You can see what you're paying per ounce, per pound, per roll, and so on. Compare the unit prices of different brands and sizes to make sure you're spending the least amount of money possible.

6. Beware of coupons. You may be able to save $1 on three rolls of brand-name tissues, but chances are great that generic brands may be cheaper than fancy labels, even with the coupon.

7. Don't always buy small. A gallon of orange juice will cost less than a quart in the long run. Even if you're single, it may make more sense for you to buy larger sizes of non-perishable groceries.

8. Don't buy what's in front of you. Less costly items often are on the top or bottom shelves. Be sure to look around before making a decision.

9. Look for items hidden in the store. The brand of black beans in the international food aisle may be more expensive than the brand of black beans you find in the canned vegetable section. Items are not necessarily grouped together, and you may find it cheaper two aisles down.

10. Buy in bulk. Bulk items often are cheaper, especially at large supermarket chains like Grand Union or outlets like Price Club.

11. Avoid convenience items. Prepared meals are going to cost you a lot. In fact, for the price of a single microwave lasagna, you can make a tray of the real thing and eat 10 meals! Don't want to eat a whole tray? Freeze some for later.

12. Buy generic or "store brand" items. There are plenty of generic items that will cost you a lot less: sugar, clothing detergent, household cleaners, paper products. Try store-brand or generic food items, too. Store-brand foods, like cheese, pasta sauce, or milk, often won't taste any different.

13. Treat yourself to a few things you love. If you stick to bare-bones bulk items, you may begin to feel

Go pastoral! Take yourself on a little vacation in the country and visit farm stands to buy fresh, inexpensive produce. It's often cheaper, and tastier, than fruit and vegetables at your supermarket. Splurge on a farm-baked cherry pie or a container of honey. If the country is too far away, find "farmers markets" held at many urban downtown areas nationwide.

The Lazy Way

deprived. Then it's just a matter of time before you blow it. Get your favorite pack of single-sliced American cheese (which is a lot cheaper when it's not individually wrapped) if you must have it.

14. When will a pint of blueberries be cheaper? December or July? It's obvious, but remember to stick to seasonal items. Berries flown in from a greenhouse or South America in winter will be a lot more expensive than berries grown locally.

15. Did you know flounder tastes the same as sole? But it costs about $7 a pound instead of $12. Ask your fish monger or butcher for low-cost cuts of meat or fish. And buy a whole chicken instead of parts. It's cheaper, and you can use the leftover for soup stock.

16. Watch the scanner at the checkout counter. Computers do make mistakes. Don't be afraid to speak up if you think they overcharged you.

17. Join a bonus-saver club. Supermarkets often give discounts to members. Bring your card with you and give it to the checkout attendant so he can give you every discount you deserve!

18. Save receipts. They'll be useful to track how much you spend and to compare with your budget.

19. Be flexible when you shop. If the supermarket has a great sale on giant boxes of your favorite cereal or pasta, get them, even if they're not on your list. Staples will keep, and they're going to cost you less than if you wait until after the sale.

A COMPLETE WASTE OF TIME

The 3 Worst Things You Can Do When Food Shopping:

1. Find out where groceries are cheapest and always shop there, even if that store is 30 miles away. (The money you save on food will be spent on gas.)

2. Always buy what's at eye-level. That's where you'll find the best priced items.

3. Shop for little things every day instead of going to the supermarket and spending more on a large quantity of food.

AN ODE TO BAKING SODA, LEMONS, AND WHITE VINEGAR

Generic or store brands are a great way to get inexpensive household items. But you may even find cheaper substitutes for costly cleaning products. White vinegar, warm water, lemon juice, and baking soda are the superheroes of cleaning products. And who wants to spend hard-earned savings on scouring products?

Mix one cup white vinegar in a bucket of hot water. It will cut the grease on your stove top, wood paneling, your floor, counters, and your coffeemaker.

Cut a lemon in half or use an open box of baking soda to deodorize your refrigerator. Lemon juice and hot water get rid of mineral stains on glassware.

Did the family pet use your new rug as a bathroom? Mix one part white vinegar with one part water, wet the stain, and blot dry. A paste of white vinegar and baking soda can remove nasty soap scum. (For more quick and easy cleaning ideas, pick up *Clean Your House The Lazy Way!*)

Keep Track of Take-Out, Dining Out, and Last-Minute Food Purchases

Get a small pad of paper or index card. Get a pen. Keep the paper and pen with you at all times. Now, start writing down when you buy food. Is it the doughnut you got before you rushed into work? The $6 lunch? Candy bars at vending machines? Drinks you charged at a bar with friends on Friday night? Energy bars at the health club? Take-out dinner? Jot down the amount you spent. No cheating! Include tips and tax. Include food you bought

YOU'LL THANK YOURSELF LATER

Buy generic staples in bulk. This could be anything from toilet paper to laundry detergent to dried pasta or rice. Bulk items often are cheaper, especially if they're a generic brand. Bulk food bins are great for items like rice, granola, or nuts that cost less when you don't buy them in expensive packaging.

IF YOU'RE SO INCLINED

Personalized coupons are starting to make their way onto your computer screen. Catalina Marketing Corp., based in St. Petersburg, FL, has developed a computer program that allows consumers to print out coupons redeemable at stores like A&P, Foodtown, Pathmark, Grand Union, Waldbaum's, and ShopRite.

One note of caution: You may be asked about your lifestyle, which means you may be giving up privacy by divulging information. Check one out at www.valupage.com.

with cash (including the 60-cent Hershey bar) as well as meals you buy with credit or diner's cards. Add the totals at the end of the day.

At the end of a week, take a look. Are you spending roughly the same amount each day. Is it $5 $13? $26? Multiply that amount by 365 days. That's what you spend in a year.

Now, ask yourself this.

"What can I get for this amount of money? What bill could I pay off?" Maybe it's time to start cutting back those food costs.

1. Eat breakfast at home. An English muffin or egg and coffee will be cheaper at home, and chances are they're a lot better for you than the cream-cheese danish you normally get on the run. (No time? Pack it up and bring it to work.)

2. Buy a coffee cup holder or thermos. Fill up at home and drink coffee en route to work if you don't have time at home.

3. Hold on to that cappuccino! Trendy coffee drinks are yummy, but for the cost of a year's worth of those triple espressos at Starbucks, you can save for a Lamborghini.

4. Is there a culinary school near you, or does the local college offer hotel management courses? Sometimes schools run top-of-the-line restaurants where you can enjoy a three-star meal for a fraction of the cost of a restaurant.

5. Restaurant servings often are big enough for two. If no one wants to share, how about digging into an appetizer for dinner? I recently ate a poached salmon salad that was a starter...for King Kong! This thing was huge! You may find it's enough to satisfy you, but half the cost of an entree.

6. Look out for prix fix dinners that include all courses instead of ordering off the menu. They could be a less expensive way to splurge.

7. Friends want to go out for dinner? How about a pot luck instead? It will be cheaper, and you won't have to wait for a table or make reservations, either!

8. Start bringing your lunch to work. The $5 to $8 you spend on take-out is costing you $100 to $120 a month! That's enough for one really great meal at a fantastic restaurant, or a good-sized payment toward your credit card.

9. Bring your own. If you absolutely have to have a bag of barbeque potato chips every afternoon, buy a big bag at the supermarket and bring a little bit to work. Two bags from a vending machine will cost about the same as a family-sized bag.

10. Start cooking your own meals (more on this later).

11. Swap homemade meals with friends. Cook a spinach quiche. Give your friend half in exchange for half of his pasta salad. You spend half the time to get two great dishes, and it won't cost as much as buying the food from a deli.

Ah, Cinderella! You're thrifty and clean! A real nineties wonder. Don't wait for Price Charming to sweep you away from all this. Put on your favorite party dress (or suit), play your favorite waltz, and call a sweetheart or friend to twirl you around the living room. Who says your castle's not your home? Especially when it's so lemony fresh!

The Lazy Way

12. Shop with a buddy. Small packages cost a lot more than family-sized portions. That means single people who buy individual-sized servings get hit especially hard at the grocery store. Well, despite what your mother says, you don't have to get married to enjoy some pleasures. If 12 rolls of toilet paper are too much, have a friend pay and take half. Same thing with economy-sized boxes of cereal.

13. Eat vegetarian—more often.

    Vegetarian meals are less expensive than dining on meat or fish. After all, a pound of lentils, rice, and veggies, especially if it's not canned or frozen, will cost a few dollars at most. Chicken, beef, and fish can cost up to $12 a pound or more, depending on the cut. So, veg out three times a week (if you're a sworn meat eater). You'll save grocery costs and besides, vegetarian meals are much healthier than burgers and fries.

14. Save containers! If you have containers (from pasta sauce, mayonnaise, and so on), you can keep leftovers instead of throwing them out. Containers are a great way to store dried goods like barley and rice, which are cheaper to buy in bulk than prepackaged.

15. Join a food cooperative or "buying club" for cheap groceries.

    Food cooperatives are a great way to save (and meet some pretty cool new friends). Members run the co-op, decide what they want to order, who will

Savor a cheap but elegant lunch. Pack a brown paper bag with leftover lasagna from last night's dinner, a linen napkin, and silver cutlery. If it's sunny, eat alfresco at the local park. Just like Tuscany!

The Lazy Way

deliver the food (or where members will pick it up), and make other organizational decisions.

That means you can pool your orders and enjoy cheaper prices by ordering in bulk. Members decide what they want to get, so it's possible to buy everything from dried foods, canned goods, organic grains, or snacks from a co-op.

Food co-ops are not only a great way to save money, they also are a great way to learn about nutrition, swap recipes with other neighbors, support organic farmers (if that's your thing), and make new friends.

Resources:

National Cooperative Business Association

1401 New York Ave. NW — Suite 1100

Washington, DC 20005-2160

(800) 636-6222

www.cooperative.org/food.html

The NCBA has a wealth of information on cooperatives for food, housing, child care, and agriculture. If you can't find a cooperative near you, why not start one? NCBA has a book on how to run a food buying club.

Directory of U.S. and Canadian Food Cooperatives

www.prarienet.org/co-op/directory.html

U.S. Department of Agriculture

Cooperative Services Program

Ag Box 3255

Washington, DC 20250-3255

(202)690-1384

IF YOU'RE SO

INCLINED

Grow your own vegetables or join a community garden if you have no idea how to get a seed to sprout. It's another inexpensive way to have fun and get fresh produce! Do you have extra zucchini? Turn it into zucchini muffins or donate some to the food bank. You may be in debt, but chances are there's someone who can use your help.

You store extra blankets in the oven. Your cupboards hold old mail, your Rollerblades™, and extra supplies of toilet paper. It's time to change that if you're going to save money and time on food. Stock your kitchen with basic cooking utensils. If you're not sure what to buy, go for the "kits" that include three different size mixing bowls, spoons, different carving knives, etc. The investment in basics will be an invaluable investment.

Check out the agency's free publication, USDA's Cooperative Service, which describes educational publications, reports, and videos you can get to learn more about food cooperatives.

WHAT YOU POSITIVELY MUST HAVE IN THE KITCHEN

There's no other way to slice it, mix it, sift it, or bake it. Cooking your own food is a lot cheaper than eating out. You don't have to be Julia Child to make food that you actually enjoy.

Throw a chicken in the oven (after you take off the wrapper), and you've got meat for cold cuts, dinner, pasta salads, omelets, or maybe the dog. Homemade soups are hearty meals in the winter, and they cost very little. A can of soup can be $2! Make your own. The more you cook, the more adventurous you may get and more skilled. And you'll be saving while you cook.

Basic Must-Have Kitchen Utensils:

- Mixing bowls
- Cooking pot with lid (one big, one small)
- Skillet
- Roasting pan
- Baking sheets
- Muffin and cake tins (disregard if you hate pastries)
- Rolling pin (doubles as security from collectors and traveling salesmen)
- Measuring cups

- Measuring spoons
- Set of knives: carving knife, serrated bread knife, 4-inch paring knife,
- Chef's knife
- Cutting board
- Whisk
- Electric mixer
- Blender or food processor
- Vegetable peeler
- Slotted spoon
- Rubber and metal spatulas
- Sieve
- Cheese grater
- Oven mitt
- Decent cookbook(s)
- Coffeemaker (if you don't like instant)
- Cutlery, plates, glasses, mugs

Where to Get Them

Fancy culinary boutiques like Williams—Sonoma have beautiful gadgets to make any kitchen look like a palace, but you pay a premium for the equipment.

Discount stores like Bradlees often have great deals on cookware. Large supermarkets often sell 99-cent specialty items like plastic ice trays. If you buy a lot of takeout, start saving plastic containers. They're just as good as Tupperware™, only free! Swap meets and street sales

IF YOU'RE SO
INCLINED

Not sure which kitchen utensils to buy first? Is a pastry bag really necessary? What about an oven thermometer? Look at recipies that you'd probably make and see which items you'd need. If you see things like "whisk" or "measure," then go for the whisk and measuring cups. Hint: Unless you have to have iced cookies and cakes covered with Boucherlike roses, you can probably survive without the pastry bag.

are a good place to pick up dish towels and other kitchen ware. Mail orders may be another good source.

Kitchen Etc.
32 Industrial Dr.
Exeter, NH 03833
(603) 773-0020

Save up to 40 percent on cutlery, china, glassware, cooking knives. Call for a free catalog.

Must-Have Ingredients:
Spices (get a spice rack that comes with the basics if you don't know what to get). Pepper, salt, oregano, parsley, garlic, cayenne pepper, bay leaves, basil, vanilla. Or go through a cookbook and look at recipes that tempt you. What spices do they use? Take note and get those.

- Cooking oil (olive oil or vegetable oil or both)
- Vinegar: white vinegar, red wine vinegar, balsamic
- Flour
- White and brown sugar
- Eggs
- Baking soda
- Baking powder

Must-Have Staples:
- Bread
- Butter
- Eggs

Congratulations! You've just outfitted your kitchen with basic ingredients and kitchen utensils. Celebrate by cooking a simple meal. Invite someone over to share it with you and dine on your accomplishment!

The Lazy Way

- Milk

- Pasta

- Pasta sauce

- Meat (keep it frozen until you're ready to use it)

- Fresh fruit and veggies

- Salad dressing

- Canned tuna fish

- Soup

- Rice, barley, grains (you can use them for stir fry, side dishes, casseroles)

Other Good Things To Make Instant-Meals:

- Jam

- Peanut butter

- Cheese

- Cereal

- Beans (black beans, garbanzo, lentils for salads, bur-ritos, soups, salads)

- Coffee, tea

Things have changed since the days when our great-grandmothers passed down their recipes to our grand-mothers. Chances are many of our moms and dads aren't just down the road to help us learn how to cook. Bookstores are crammed with great cookbooks, and many of the volumes are sold at a discount. Here are some good books to start you off if you barely know how to boil water or need basic guides to get you started.

IF YOU'RE SO
INCLINED

Afraid of using your newly stocked kitchen? Ease the pressure with comfort food. Invite friends over to share a feast you make of your favorite childhood recipes: peanut-butter sandwiches, mashed potatoes, waffles, and butterscotch pudding.

You don't have to enroll in the Culinary Institute of America to learn how to bake, grill, chop, or mix. Community colleges, recreation centers, or other campuses often have semester or day-long courses where you can learn the basics or master the art of pastry making. The investment in a class may pay off in the long run.

Cook Your Meals The Lazy Way, by Sharon Bowers, Macmillan.

The quick and easy way to get good food on the table fast.

Recipes 1-2-3: Fabulous Food Using Only 3 Ingredients, by Rozanne Gold, Viking Press

Comes with beautiful color photographs, and you'll be amazed how "gourmet" these simple, fast meals can look and taste!

Moosewood Cookbook, by Mollie Katzen, 10 Speed Press.

A bible among vegetarians for years, but recipes like Polenta Pie, Vegetarian Tostadas, and Carrot Cake have tempted carnivores, too.

Jessica's Biscuit: The Cookbook People
Box 301
Newtonville, MA 02160
(800) 878-4264

A toll-free call for a free catalog of cookbooks that are 45 to 80 percent off. Returns accepted. Need we say more?

Ask a Friend for Help

Do you sniff madly when you pass by your neighbor's door? Be neighborly. Maybe you can barter a cooking lesson for something you do. (Can you type out a report? Are you great with houseplants? How about walking their dog or baby-sitting?)

Getting Money on Your Side

	The Old Way	The Lazy Way
Stir-fry veggies	$8 takeout	About $2 homemade
Chicken dinner	$4 for 1 microwavable	$4 for the whole chicken
Sandwich lunch	$6 at deli	$1 to $2 homemade
Breakfast on the run	$1.50 for coffee and bagel at the deli	Pennies for coffee and bagel brought from home

Chapter eight

Style and Flash Without Spending the Cash

You remember the day you learned that the mythical Golden Fleece didn't come from Brooks Brothers, and a banana republic is a disparaging political expression. What a shock! Life beyond fashion!

You live for beauty, and your bills show it. Last month's credit-card bill looks like a who's who of outlets and fashion houses: Bloomingdale's—where you stocked up at the Lancome, Estee Lauder, and Aveda counters—Banana Republic, Saks Fifth Avenue, Versace, Ralph Lauren, and the Gap.

Speaking of gaps, have you seen the one in your budget? You're so broke, you still haven't finished paying for the fake leopard coat you bought five years ago, when you just "had to have" faux. Controlling what you spend on your clothing and personal items won't mean you'll look out of style. In fact, you may be surprised at how many great finds you'll come across without rushing out to chic boutiques the day new fall collections hit the racks. You do, however, need some

restraint, lots of creativity, some courage to try your hand at sewing your own, and faith that you can look your best without going bankrupt.

SAMPLE SALES

Want a designer wardrobe but can't afford the prices? Designers often sell prototypes of their new lines—called samples—at their showrooms. Sample sales are not advertised or well-known by the public, but they're not impossible to find. Moreover, they are fantastic treasure troves of inexpensive but high-quality clothing. It's not uncommon for slinky dresses or sweaters to sell for a tenth of their retail price.

Of course, you can't expect to find a full range of sizes in every style that catches your fancy. Yet the steep discounts make sample sales all-around terrific bargains that are worth tracking down.

The Internet has two great sites to find where the best sales, including sample sales, are being held nationwide.

www.samplesale.com
Run by:
Home on the Web
40 E. 12th St.
New York, NY 10003
(212) 565-3576

This fantastic site can get you free information about sample sales held in New York City, Miami, Los Angeles, San Francisco, Washington, D.C., Boston, and Chicago.

In addition to sample sale information, you'll find a monthly calendar of the best sales at boutiques, and there's an easy link to get on e-mail lists from your favorite designers:

www.findasale.com

Want to know where you can buy inexpensive clothes, linens, housewares, or find information about specific designers at stores in your neighborhood? Then this is the site, which has information about clothing stores nationwide. Questions about Findasale? Call (212) 55-SALES.

Manhattan is one of the world's premier fashion capitals, and luckily it's getting easier to track down showrooms in the city's garment district where you can find sample sales that are normally "best-kept secrets" among the fashion elite.

Fashion Information Booth
39th Street at 7th Ave.
New York, NY 10018
Hours: Monday–Friday 10 a.m. to 4 p.m.
(212) 398-7943

Run by the Fashion Center Business Improvement District, the information booth is run by experts who can answer any question you may have about Manhattan's fashion houses. Find out where to track down your favorite designer showroom and get the inside scoop on sample sales.

IF YOU'RE SO
INCLINED

It's mind-boggling what people forget at dry cleaners. But sometimes, proprietors sell the clothing if it's been taking up room in their shops for too long. Ask around to see if any forgotten items are for sale. In other words, don't get taken to the cleaners, but go!

IF YOU'RE SO INCLINED

You have new clothes but what about the items you no longer want? Why not give anything that is clean, pressed, and usable to charity to help someone out who has even less than you? Be sure to get a receipt for your donation. You can use it to make a charitable tax deduction. After all, every old coat has a silver lining.

S&B Report
Lazar Media Group, Inc.
108 E. 38th St.
New York, NY 10016
(212) 683-7613

This monthly insider newsletter lists 50 to 250 designers in the New York area. A year's subscription to *S&B* costs $49, but the plethora of information on sample sales makes the subscription a worthwhile investment for many.

Sample sales are certainly not exclusive to New York. The Windy City also is a fashionable city. To find out more about local Chicago designers and sample sales, contact:

The Apparel Industry Board
350 N. Orleans St., Room 1047
Chicago, IL 60654
(312) 836-1041

CONSIGNMENT AND THRIFT SHOPS

Some of the world's most fashionable people have relied on great finds at these second-hand stores. Where else can you find off-beat dresses, leather jackets, or fancy tuxedos and top hats from the 1920s without paying a fortune?

The shops also are a great place to sell or trade some of your clothes for a new look. You don't have to buy.

Consignment and thrift shops often reflect their neighborhood. Need inexpensive work clothes? Then hit a consignment shop in a more conservative part of town.

Want a slinky velvet dress from the 1930s? Go to Greenwich Village (or the equivalent) near you.

THE FIVE COMMANDMENTS OF SMART SHOPPING

1. Thou Shalt Know When to Shop

   If you absolutely need to get it new, try to take advantage of sales seasons. (There is more than one.) Here's a general guideline.

   January: After-Christmas sales and winter clothing goes on sale.

   April: Sales on rain gear and spring outfits.

   July: This is a great time to get inexpensive bathing suits; summer clothing goes on sale to make room for fall and winter clothing.

   December: Formal party attire and coats go on sale, and if you can stand the crowds, hit the pre-Christmas sales when stores begin to panic about getting rid of their merchandise.

2. Thou Shalt Not Shop Without a List

   If you just wander into stores, you'll be seized with a sudden urge to own lizard-skin cowboy boots and a blue suede suit. Know what you absolutely need and buy only those items.

3. Thou Shalt Shop with Cash

   Remember that nasty credit-card bill that's been causing you so much trouble? Chances are you won't

YOU'LL THANK YOURSELF LATER

Are you and your friends tired of your wardrobes? Pool your tired old threads together for a swap day. Make sure everyone brings clean, repaired clothes so you don't get dumped with a bunch of old rags. Put on some great music, serve drinks and snacks, and make a party out of getting great, almost-new clothes!

be able to resist using it if you bring it shopping. Sticking to cash on hand also means you won't spend what you don't have.

4. Thou Shalt Shun Trendy Clothing

Trendy clothing goes out of style quickly. That's why it's trendy. Invest your limited resources on quality, traditional clothes that can be worn for more than a season. And make sure you stick to colors—greys, blues, blacks, creams, browns—so that you can mix and match as many outfits as possible.

5. Thou Shalt Be a Patient Shopper

You didn't really think you needed those shoes, but it was love at first sight. Then again, it could be lust. To find out how true your heart is, wait three days before you consider buying them. If your footsies are still screaming for those stilettos, if you can afford to buy them without using the credit card, and if you can wear them with clothing you already own, then get them.

Discount Stores and Outlet Malls

Not all stores are created equal. Some are much more expensive than others. But be wary of stores that always advertise big discounts. Chances are they've just marked up the price so they can "cut" it, and your sale won't really be a sale. If you can go into stores and compare prices before you buy (don't try this unless you know you'll be disciplined), then you can really be sure you're getting the best deals around.

There are plenty of great stores to take advantage of great buys:

Loehmans: everything from suits to socks, dresses, blouses, jackets, and more

Filene's Basement: all types of clothing

T.J. Maxx: great for teenagers

Army/Navy Stores: low-priced pants, outdoor gear, rain wear

TAKE CARE OF WHAT YOU HAVE

It sounds obvious, but taking care of your clothing will prolong its life. Read care instructions carefully, and follow them! If you throw that cashmere sweater in the dryer, you're going to be very sorry. If you get new shoes, have a thin, protective rubber sole and heel put on them to prolong their life. Cover suede with a protective spray, available at any shoe store. Repair holes on jeans before they get too big. A little love and attention will keep you from going threadbare and broke.

Get Your Kids' Clothes at Swap Shops

Children outgrow clothes very quickly. But ask other parents, check your Yellow Pages, or ask local child-care experts (nannies, nursery schools) if they know of any consignment shops for children's clothes. It's a great way to trade or sell the clothes your kids have outgrown, and you can get second-hand items for far less than new toddler togs.

QUICK ●—● PAINLESS

The first time you wash new colored clothes, throw in a quarter cup of white vinegar in the wash. It will help set colors and keep them from fading or looking old.

Scrutinize Your Clothing Catalogs, Then Pounce!

If you're like most of us, your mailbox gets stuffed with clothing catalogs. If you're really broke, don't look at them and remove all temptation. If you need something and you think a catalog will have good buys, wait a week or two. Mail-order businesses like Eddie Bauer and Victoria's Secret often send "sale" catalogs a few weeks after they mail their originals, and you'll find the exact same items at 10 to 50 percent off.

SEW YOUR OWN

At the very least, you should know how to sew buttons back on clothing, darn a sock, and put a patch over a hole in your jeans. But if you make the effort to sew items from scratch, you'll have an unlimited wardrobe in your future.

Ask friends—or your grandma—if they can teach you how. There are books at the library that can guide you through the basics. Or check your local recreation center, sewing shop, or community college for inexpensive classes. The cost of tuition may save you thousands of dollars in the long run.

Must Have's for Basic Sewing Repairs:

- Needles
- Pins
- Thread (blue, brown, black, grey, white)
- Sewing scissors
- Tape measure

IF YOU'RE SO
INCLINED

Tired of your pale yellow dress? Do you have a stain on your white jeans? Dye them a different color and get a brand new outfit for just a few dollars.

More Handy Sewing Tools If You're Going to Make Your Own:

- Sewing machine
- Large table to work and spread out fabric (dinner table will do)
- Sewing chalk
- Stitch ripper

PRICE-CONSCIOUS PERSONAL AND BEAUTY ITEMS

Beauty can be a lot of things, but it always costs something. Even Cleopatra had to shop for the kohl around her eyes. But you don't have to be an Egyptian empress to look like royalty.

Hair

Free or low-cost hair care. Beauty salons like Vidal Sassoon Salon or Jean-Louis David often have student night where you can get free cuts, permanents, and coloring. Call and ask if your favorite salon offers these inexpensive perks.

Stockings with runs can be turned into hair bands. Cut the legs into one-inch wide rings and use them to hold your locks into a neat ponytail.

Makeup

You don't have to spend money on new lipstick to find out if the color will look good on you. Cosmetics counters are a great place to get free makeovers so you can see

IF YOU'RE SO
INCLINED

You want to sew, but machines cost a couple hundred dollars. But second-hand machines can be a lot cheaper. Scout classified ads in your newspaper or put up a "wanted" sign at local sewing stores alerting local seamstresses and tailors that you're looking for a good deal. If you've never sewn, ask the seller to demonstrate and make sure the machine comes with its original instructions.

If you don't have money, don't go into stores. You'll only make yourself miserable by the temptations. Instead, spoil yourself to a free treat. Go to a free play in the park or the museum. Enjoy a picnic with a friend. Borrow videos and watch classics.

The Lazy Way

what works before you buy.

Ask for freebies. If you spend money at cosmetics counters, ask if they have any samples you can have. After all, they'll want your business, and they hope that if you like the products, you'll come back and spend more money.

Returns. Rite Aid sells inexpensive products. But even if you buy the wrong brand or color, you can take it back. Save your receipt!

Don't be a label hound. Sure, you can spend nearly $20 on a tube of mascara, but there are many products sold for a quarter of the cost at the local pharmacy. Chain stores, like CVS, Cosmetics Plus, and Rite Aid, have great deals. If you're not sure whether or not a generic beauty aid is the same as a name-brand item, compare the ingredient labels.

Lotions and Potions

There are plenty of beauty products you can make from items you have in your pantry. These low-cost alternatives are a great way to pamper yourself without spending a mint. Here are a few:

Baking Soda Scrub: Mix 2 tablespoons baking soda, 2 tablespoon ground rice powder, and 1 teaspoon grated lemon peel. Mix and scrub.

Bran and Oatmeal Scrub: Mix 1 cup bran, 1 cup oatmeal, and 2 tablespoons milk. Scrub those dead skin cells away and enjoy a healthy glow.

Natural Foot Pumice: Walk on a beach and rub those feet nice and smooth.

Getting Money on Your Side

	The Old Way	The Lazy Way
Haircut	$40 to $60 at salon	$0 to $15 during salon's student night
Work clothes	$300 and up for new suits	$30 for a used suit at the consignment shop
New summer skirt	$40 and up at department stores and boutiques	$10 for material if you sew your own
Soothing facial scrub	$30 from the fancy-schmancy spa	$1 from your kitchen cupboards

Vehicle Expenses That Won't Drive You Around the Bend

Unless you're driving into the sunset en route to a honeymoon (or away from your ex), owning a vehicle can be a very expensive grind. With car loans, lease payments, gas, repairs, tune-ups, new tires, city garage fees, tolls, and insurance, it would be faster to throw a couple hundred dollars in the front seat and just burn it.

Yet sprawling lives make transportation a necessary expense for many of us, whether or not we drive or take public transportation. What makes this predicament even more onerous is the fact that it often seems that except for those $1.99 pine-scented tree deodorizers hanging from your rearview mirror, there never seems to be an affordable transportation expense.

When did tires cost more than a month's salary? And can you really trust your mechanic who assures you that it's normal to replace your car battery every six months? (If you answered yes, you're definitely a sucker—a very broke sucker!)

Our haste and willing ignorance make us more vulnerable than a pot of honey in a bear's lair. It also leaves us financially drained. One Department of Transportation study estimates that a whopping 53 percent of auto repair costs are unnecessary—that's worth $20 to $40 billion per year on wasteful repairs. Knowledge, a full-tank of skepticism, and knowing where to get a better deal can save you from getting mowed down by transportation costs. And even if you don't own a vehicle and rely on someone else to get you here and there, you'll probably be able to save a few dollars, too.

BUYING A CAR ON A BATTERED BUDGET

Can you say *unctuous*? Can you say *polyester*? Can you say *shark*? Even if your automobile salesman wears 100 percent wool, has the face of a cherub, and weeps at the sight of small animals—beware!

Car sales staffers are professionals who spend hours every week earning their living by making you spend as much as possible. And unless you're Elvis Presley with a private line of cars, planes (the good ol' Lisa Marie!), and golf carts, chances are you'll need all the help and preparation you can get in obtaining the best deal for yourself.

You'll save thousands of dollars if you take the time to know what you're talking about before you even step

one foot onto the showroom floor. That means doing some homework about unpublicized deals, obtaining financing early, and knowing if rustproofing, extended warrantees, and other products are a waste of money or a good buy.

Know Your Salesperson Before You Open Your Wallet

There are a few standard rules of nature. Oil and water don't mix. Men don't see dust bunnies under the couch. And car salespeople—well, they don't want to save you money. The more you spend, the more they make. If you understand this basic concept, you'll keep your guard up when it comes time to buy a car. But there are a few other rules you should be aware of.

Know About the Car You Want Before You Shop

Friends can tell you if they've had good luck with their truck or car. But you'd be a fool not to read auto reviews for new and used cars.

Consumer Reports new and used car guides are great resources, but there are lots of others. Edmund's car guides, printed and sold in bookstores (some information is available online), also are great, and the California publisher has solid advice on ways to avoid costly traps at the dealership.

Rental agencies often sell cars after a season or two. It's a great way to get automobiles (or trucks) that are well cared for without paying too much. Call your local rental agencies toward the end of the year, when they're

A COMPLETE WASTE OF TIME

The 3 Worst Things to Do When Buying a Car:

1. Trust a salesman to sell you the best car for your budget.

2. Buy a car that matches your favorite outfit.

3. Believe that owning a Porsche will make women suddenly hurl their supine bodies in your path.

making room for new model vehicles, and find out if you can get a great deal.

Preparing to Haggle and Deal

Car dealerships may be the only places in the country, besides flea markets, where you're expected to negotiate the price. That's why it's a good idea to understand how manufacturers and dealerships set prices. Think about the following before you go car shopping, and you'll be more likely to get the best deal.

■ Never, ever pay the sticker price!

The sticker price may not reflect the cost to the dealer, and in fact, it may be inflated. Base your offer on the dealer invoice cost, and you may be able to pay less than that figure.

■ Use the dealer invoice cost to start negotiating.

This is what the dealer is billed for a new vehicle to get delivered to his or her showroom. But it may not be what the dealer pays for the car because the dealer gets other breaks from the manufacturer.

You can obtain dealer invoice costs from a variety of sources, including the Kelley *Blue Book* and Edmund's vehicle guides

■ Be aware of other breaks your salesperson may be getting but not sharing!

Holdback costs: This is the amount the manufacturer pays back to the dealer after the car is sold. So, even if you buy the car at invoice, your salesperson probably is making $500 on the sale because of holdbacks.

You'll Be Glad You Did

If you know what perks and bonuses your car dealership will make when you buy a car, you'll be in a much better position to figure out how little you can get away with paying. Chances are the dealership won't tell you about holdback costs or other incentives. But you can find out from a few sources. You can check out the Edmund's car guides to see how much the dealer paid for the vehicle and what kind of incentives and rebates they're getting (www.edmunds.com).

- End of Year Sales:

  Dealerships have to fill sales quotas, and they must get rid of old stock at the end of the year. As a result, you're more likely to negotiate a better price for yourself.

- Factory to Dealer Incentives:

  When there's an overabundance of a particular make or model, or when manufacturers are gearing up for new models to roll off the assembly line, they'll pay dealers money for selling particular cars or trucks they want to get rid of. Sometimes the incentives are advertised, but many times they're not.

- The "F&I" Guys:

  The finance and insurance (F&I) department makes its commissions based on how much you spend. As a result, you'll be persuaded to buy everything from the car loan and rustproofing to extended warrantees. Some of these products are worth it, and some aren't. But nearly all will cost a bundle, and chances

If you need to borrow cash for your new wheels, do it before you go shopping. You'll keep yourself on a tight budget if you select a vehicle to fit your expense account rather than getting a loan that's big enough to pay for that monster truck you didn't realize you wanted until you went for a test drive. By getting a loan early, you also can shop around for the lowest interest rates and save, too.

are you'll be able to save if you buy them somewhere else.

Car Loans and Financing

Financing a car through the dealership is sure to be a colossal waste of money. In fact, the F&I salesperson is just that, a salesperson who stands to profit on what you spend. The loan and interest rate he tracks for you from a bank could be padded. If you know you can get a loan from a credit union or bank at 6.7 percent, you can make the salesperson match that price or do better.

Extended Warrantees

New cars come with good warranties that generally cover up to three years or 36,000 miles. Don't get the extended warranty if you're not planning to keep the car for a few years or if the car has a good repair history. However, if you're planning to keep the car for a long time, the warranty may be a good idea.

You should buy the extended coverage from a third party like an insurance agent. Mark Eskeldson, author of *What Car Dealers Don't Want You to Know*, recommends that a good deal costs no more than $1,000 with a $50 deductible per visit, not per item. On new cars, he says the warranty should run six years and 75,000 miles. Used cars should be covered for two years or 24,000 miles.

Rustproofing, Seat Protection, Alarms, and So On

- Rust proofing is a waste of money considering that most warranties cover corrosion.

- Seat Protection. Another big waste of a couple hundred dollars. Buy a can of Scotchguard™ and spray your own seat, or cover the car seat with a sheet or blanket that you can throw in the wash when it gets dirty.

- Alarms. You have to decide if you live in a place where an alarm is worth it, but chances are great that you'll save money if you have an alarm installed by an independent car alarm company instead of the dealership.

Remember Your Trade-In Is Worth Money!

If you pick out your new car then begin to negotiate the value of your trade-in, you're likely to give it away for nothing, says Lev Stark, vice president of Edmund's Publications, the car buyers' guides. Stark recommends that you find out the value of your trade-in *before* you shop for a new car. You can look at the Edmund's Used-Car guides or the Kelley *Blue Book* guides for this information.

Leasing Is Usually a Losing Proposition

Leasing is generally a big waste of money unless you're planing to trade in a car every few years, and you don't expect to drive much. Some consumers can get better deals on leasing used (which are sometimes called "offlease") vehicles. Ask your dealership if they have them.

If you want to learn more about leasing and some of the jargon you'll need to wade through, see leasesource.com, an online source of great lease information: www.leasesource.com.

QUICK **PAINLESS**

Spray fabric or other protection on the seats of your new car the day you get it and put mats on the floors. A little protection can prolong the look, wear, and worth of your new vehicle.

TEN-TIPS ON BUYING A USED VEHICLE (COMPLIMENTS OF *Consumer Reports*)

1. Look for mismatched paint on body panels that may indicate whether or not the vehicle has been in an accident. In other words, if it has a Cadillac bumper, a Nova rear, and Volkswagen doors, it's not a good buy.

2. Check for rust on doors, under the carpeting, and inside the trunk. If it has spread too far, the car may be too old, and too expensive, to fix.

3. Look for water leaks around glass and water stains on the vehicle upholstery.

4. Look under the car and check for drips. If you find oil, gas, transmission and brake fluid, or engine coolant, it's probably a bad buy.

5. Make sure all the lights and dashboard controls work.

6. When you turn on the ignition, make sure the "check engine" light comes on. If it doesn't, it may indicate that the bulb was removed to cover up a problem with the engine.

7. Drive on a level road to make sure the vehicle doesn't pull to one side.

8. In a safe place (parking lot, empty street), step on the brakes hard. The car should stop straight and not pull to any side. Oh yeah, the car should also stop.

9. Turn the car on, and while the engine is idling, pull the dipstick from the automatic transmission. If there is any burned smell or bubbles, the transmission is bad.

10. Check your tail. When you drive, accelerate to 15 mph, then release the accelerator and slow down to 5 mph. Push the accelerator again. If a cloud of blue smoke comes from the tailpipe as you accelerate, the engine could be burning oil.

Some Helpful Resources

What Car Dealers Don't Want You to Know, by Mark Eskeldson, Technews Publishing.

Eskeldson's book should be a must-read car bible for anyone buying or leasing new and used cars. Eskeldson has the inside scoop on scams, bonuses, ways to save money, insurance, warranties, and more. He's also written *What Auto Mechanics Don't Want You to Know*.

Edmund's Publications Corp.

P.O. Box 18827

Beverly Hills, CA 90209-4827

(310) 278-8301

www.edmunds.com

Kelley *Blue Book*

P.O. Box 19651

Irvine, CA 92643

www.kbb.com

YOU'LL THANK YOURSELF LATER

Don't panic if you absolutely need a car to get to work, but you have only $500 to spend. You may be able to get a good deal from the government (of all places!). Cities, towns, and villages often auction used or seized goods, including cars from their police or public works departments. The vehicle you buy won't come with guarantees, and you're taking a bit of a risk, but if you're really broke and immobile, the wheels may carry you long enough for you to save for a better car.

The used-car guide is another old bible for consumers. Issues are released twice a year, in January and July. They are available in bookstores, or you can order them.

Consumer Reports
20 Academy St.
Norwalk, CT 06852-7100
www.consumerreports.org

Consumer Reports—both in print and online—has information about used and new cars and about auto insurance. The annual April buyers' guide and the organization's yearly survey of 4.5 million drivers on used cars are fantastic.

The Complete Idiot's Guide to Buying or Leasing a Car, by Jack R. Nerard, Alpha Books.

UNSURE ABOUT AUTOMOBILE INSURANCE?

Somehow, buying automobile insurance is akin to thinking about our own funerals. Both are necessary, but grisly expenses. Who wants to think about getting into an accident or having your shiny new sportscar chopped and quartered like the Thanksgiving turkey and then sold for parts? Then there's convoluted insurance lingo. Reading engine schematics is more interesting—and easier to understand—than many insurance agreements.

Consumer Reports estimates that American drivers spend more than $300 million more than they need to on insurance each year. Chances are you're one of those people wasting money. Yet once again, a few phone calls and comparison shopping, and knowing the basics about insurance, can go a long way in helping you steer clear of costly insurance dead ends.

■ **Rule One:** Don't buy your auto insurance from the first guy you talk to.

You have money. Insurance companies want it. Make them work for it. Experts recommend you survey at least six insurance vendors. You can buy your coverage from direct sellers like Geico, who sell you insurance without a middleman and give quotes over the phone. Or you can go to insurance agents who act as a go-between between you and independent insurance companies.

Who Has the Best Insurance Deals?

There's no hard and fast rule on where you can save the most. Sometimes big-name companies like State Farm or the Automobile Association of America (AAA) have the best bets, and sometimes it's the smaller vendors. Sample a variety of places because you'll never know who can offer the lowest price.

What you spend depends largely on you. Insurance companies use a host of information to determine a quote, ranging from your driving experience and record to your gender, age, home address, and the make and model of your car. Younger drivers generally will pay more than older, presumably more experienced and

YOU'LL THANK YOURSELF LATER

Don't risk everything you're worth by skimping or doing without auto insurance. Many states require insurance, and it's expensive to get caught without it. Worse, if you hit or hurt someone, you could be paying for life if you don't have insurance to cover your costs.

cautious drivers. Some check credit reports, so make sure yours is in good standing (review chapter 1 on credit reports).

A REALLY GOOD FAST 'N' EASY INSURANCE RESOURCE

If you don't have the time to call and survey insurance companies for the best rates, you may be able to use Consumer Reports Auto Insurance Price Service. For $12 (add $8 for additional vehicles) and about 10 minutes over the phone, they'll get you a list of 25 insurance quotes determined on your driving information.

The service is available in Arizona, California, Colorado, Connecticut, Florida, Georgia, Illinois, Louisiana, New Jersey, Michigan, Missouri, Nevada, New York, Ohio, Pennsylvania, Tennessee, Texas, Virginia, Washington (state), and Wisconsin.

These folks figure they've saved the average customer $400 a year. But the best part of all, the call is free: (800) 807-8050.

▓ **Rule Two:** Protect yourself before you protect your car

Your insurance agreement includes different types of protection, and what you spend ultimately depends on how much coverage you get.

First, know what the coverage means.

Comprehensive—Covers costs to repair a vehicle that is damaged by acts of God, like earthquakes and falling tree branches.

Collision—Covers damage to your car if you crash it.

Liability—Protects you if you are ever sued and lose.

Medical—Covers medical costs to you for auto accident injuries.

Collision and Comprehensive—This option explains why insurance companies can waste money!

Generally, try to go for a big deductible (the amount you pay out of your pocket before the insurance company pays for damage) for comprehensive and collision insurance. The bigger your deductible, the less you'll pay on insurance. At a minimum, have a $500 deductible. If you can save for a rainy day, go for a $1,000 deductible on comprehensive and collision.

If your car is worth less than $4,000, consider dropping both collision and comprehensive. You may find that it's really not worth it in the long run.

Liability—Why It Pays to Spend More

Protect yourself, not the car! It's better to have more liability to protect you in case of a lawsuit than the car.

Think about it. If your $12,000 sedan is totaled, that hurts. But what about if you're sued (and lose) an $80,000 or $200,000 lawsuit? You'd be in a financial hole for many, many years—possibly your entire life. *Consumer Reports* recommends you get no less than $100,000 per person or $300,000 per accident. If you want more liability protection but want to keep your total insurance costs low, then raise the deductible on the comprehensive and collision coverage.

YOU'LL THANK YOURSELF LATER

Don't have time to pour over insurance offers? Remember this rule. Protect yourself, not your car! Make sure you have enough liability coverage (minimally, $300,000 an accident) and cut back on collision and comprehensive coverage if you need to keep your total tab within limits.

The 3 Worst Things to Do
When Getting Car
Insurance:

1. Get medical insurance
   in your auto coverage
   if you're already pro-
   tected under a differ-
   ent plan.

2. Buy automobile insur-
   ance without asking
   for discounts for being
   a good customer or
   you're renewing your
   policy.

3. Purchase automobile
   insurance if you ride a
   bike.

Medical Insurance—When It's a Waste and When It's a Good Deal

If you're covered in another policy that's good, you probably don't need the coverage. The same thing is true if
you don't use your vehicle a lot. But if you're self-
employed, drive great distances, or have skimpy medical
insurance, it's good to buy.

Rule Three: Ask for discounts

There are times in life when it's best not to ask for more,
such as hitting your honey up for a bigger diamond on
the engagement ring. Major faux pas! Then there are
times to be like Oliver Twist and ask for more. Buying
insurance is one of those times to be pushy. Insurance
companies often don't advertise discounts, but you can
get them by asking. Don't forget to say "please" and be
polite. After all, who wants to help a nasty grouch?

Renewal Discounts—Have you been with an insurance company for a while, and do you have a good
record? Ask for a discount when it's time to renew
your policy. Make sure you're getting preferred rates.

Defensive Driving Discounts—No, this doesn't mean
driving in a fit of catatonic rage as you try to get
around Miss Daisy puttering along in the fast lane.
Defensive (or safe) driving courses may entitle you
to insurance discounts if you have learned to curb
your temper and have refreshed your memory on
the difference between the yellow and green light
(hint: yellow does not mean blow through the inter-
section).

Ask your local Department of Motor Vehicles or your current (and prospective) insurance companies if they offer the defensive driving breaks. If they do, they'll have lists of local schools that offer the safety classes. Note that the classes are available to motorcycle drivers, too.

- Good Driver Discounts—If you're lucky enough to have a clean record, ask if you qualify for any preferred driver rates.

- Combined Coverage Discounts—It may be cheaper to insure a vehicle if you combine it with insurance for other things like a boat or by putting it with your homeowner's insurance.

VEHICLE REPAIRS AND COST-SAVING TIPS TO GET FROM HERE TO THERE

Five Quick Rules to Stay Out of Trouble:

1. Make sure any repair you make is covered by your warranty before you pay out of your own pocket to replace or repair worn parts.

2. In general, follow guidelines in your manufacturer's handbook on tune-ups and repairs.

3. If repairs are covered by the warranty, then go to an authorized dealership, or you may end up paying the tab. However, dealerships tend to cost more than independent garages for repairs that are not covered by warranties. Finding a reputable mechanic can be tricky. There is no formula. Ask around, and if you find someone you trust, stick with him.

All this talk about insurance can make even the hardiest person shudder in fear. Crumpled metal. Stolen cars. Crushed motorcycles. After you've gone over your insurance policy, reassure yourself and get rid of those jitters. Play soothing music. Ask a friend for a hug or a soothing back rub. Tell yourself, "I'm OK." It's true, especially now that you've saved some cash by shopping around for the best insurance deal around!

The Lazy Way

4. Get any estimate in writing!

5. Keep all receipts from repairs and warranties to protect yourself if you find you've broken down again.

For example, don't just let a mechanic tell you that you need new belts. Is that timing belts? Does that mean the valves need to be cleaned and removed of carbon, which builds up because of combustion? What other parts will be replaced? How much will this cost?

Then, with this knowledge, get a second opinion without telling the new mechanic you were told you need new belts. If he reaches the same conclusion, find out what his estimate includes. If he neglects to mention the valves being cleaned, say "hey, what about the valves?" They'll know you're not an idiot who can be easily taken for a ride. Call at least three different places to make sure you get the best deal.

SOME MAINTENANCE TIPS

Tires:

- Keep tires full of air as directed by the manufacturer guidelines. You'll save on gas mileage.

- Buy a tire pressure gauge and keep it in the glove compartment where it's handy so you can fill your tires yourself. It's easy to do and a waste of money to pay someone else to do it.

- Do without the fancy white-walls and costly tires. Shop around and get quotes on the best price or check out stores like Price Club for low-priced wheels.

Oil:

- You can change your oil every 7,500 miles, not 3,000, and make sure the garage has changed your old filter. Ask to see the old one. Don't neglect to change the oil, however—it keeps the engine running smoothly and prolongs the life of your car.

Brakes:

- Calipers can last up to 100,000 miles, so make sure you don't get talked into new ones unless you need them, or you'll wind up paying a couple hundred dollars.

Mufflers:

- Federal law requires that catalytic converters in vehicles older than 1995 have to be covered by five-year, 50,000-mile warranties. Cars built after then must have eight-year and 80,000-mile coverage. Make sure you don't pay for a new converter if your car is still covered.

BATTERIES, ALTERNATORS, AND GENERATORS

Invest in jumper cables. It's only a matter of time before you leave the lights on and your battery needs to be recharged. If you have the cables, you can get a jump start from anyone without paying for a tow company, and it will be faster than waiting for a mechanic to show up.

Here's the good news; it's easy to jump a battery. Remember: Red cable goes on the positive (which should be marked on the battery with a plus sign), black on

IF YOU'RE SO
INCLINED

Check with your Better Business Bureau and your state's Department of Consumer Affairs to make sure there are no claims against a garage or mechanic you're about to hire to replace your engine.

Some bits of paper should be thrown away but not warranties for car parts or repairs. If something goes wrong, you can get a replacement part. Moreover, it's often easier to get a higher price for your vehicle when you sell it if you can show records proving you've kept your car or truck on a regular tune-up schedule. Keep the warranty for your battery. If the battery goes dead before the warranty date, you should get it replaced for free!

negative. Don't let the cable ends touch each other when they're connected to an idling engine! Read all jumper cable warnings and mechanic's handbook before you do this. Make sure you don't get charged for a new alternator or generator if your battery is bad. An alternator can cost more than a couple hundred dollars. A battery is $30 to $60. An alternator and voltage regulator test for about $30 will let you know whether these charging systems are working, or if it's just a battery.

Radios

Driving in silence can drive all of us nuts, especially when we're sitting in traffic or worrying about the bills. But car stereos can be expensive. An independent shop specializing in car stereos probably will be less costly than the dealership. Get a quote before you get a new car to make sure you can buy it for less somewhere else or demand that the dealer match your good price. You can even order one through the mail through a place like Crutchfield Corp. (800) 955-9009, which will send you step-by-step instructions.

DO YOUR OWN WORK

Doing basic repairs and changing your oil can save you a bundle. Read your manufacturer's handbook or get books on auto repair (such as *Take Care of Your Car The Lazy Way*). Look for step-by-step instructions to make sure you don't wind up with three extra lug nuts on your garage floor when you're done changing the tires.

Invest in these handy tools to keep you running:

- Flashlight
- Tire pressure gauge
- Spare tire that is properly filled (you don't know the meaning of "bummer" until you're stuck in the middle of nowhere with a flat tire and a flat spare)
- Flares in case you're in an accident
- Gas can and siphon to get gas if you run dry
- Jumper cables

SIMPLE COST-SAVERS FOR DRIVERS AND VETERANS OF PUBLIC TRANSPORTATION

- Slow down and save on fuel costs.

  Your lead foot is costing you money. Follow the speed limit, leave a few extra minutes to get to work, and slow down. You'll burn less gas.

- Take the load of bricks out of your trunk.

  Lighten your load and boost your fuel efficiency. If you have a vehicle filled with heavy materials, get rid of them. (Your big brother doesn't count.)

- Drive an efficient car.

  Those popular sport utility vehicles can get you through a war or up a rocky mountain, but face it, you're just driving to the mall and work. You don't need to drive that turbo-charged, cup-holder-laden assault vehicle that guzzles a gallon of gas every 12 or 13 miles. Consider this: Gas prices are roughly 46 cents a mile. Look at your odometer and see how far

IF YOU'RE SO
INCLINED

You can barely screw in a new light bulb, so the thought of repairing the simplest thing on your car or refilling windshield wiper fluid is out of the question. That doesn't mean you have to spend a lot. Go for bartering. Maybe your neighbor changes his own oil and would be willing to help you in exchange for a batch of homemade cookies or getting his lawn cut. Be creative and look for people who can help you at a price, or swap, you can afford.

you go in a week. Is it worth the expense to have an inefficient car? Go for vehicles with great gas mileage, and you'll save in the long run.

- Consider joining the Automobile Association of America (AAA).

  AAA members can get a plethora of free services, like roadside towing, a helping hand if you lock yourself out, and free maps. Check your local telephone listing for a "Triple-A" office nearest you, or call their national headquarters in Heathrow, Florida: (407) 444-8000.

- Carpool—Take turns carpooling with colleagues from your office or neighbors who work in the same city. Some places, like Oakland, California, have carpool stations at local bus stops and gas stations. Cars pull up, and passengers pile in until there are three people. It saves money, and you get to use those speedy HOV lanes.

- Improve your bottom and your bottom line—Walk, bike, or in-line skate to work.

- Buy toll tickets in bulk and save—Many tolls, bridges, and pass-through gates sell books of tickets or electronic passes that give you price breaks.

- Stop hailing taxicabs—A cab ride is expensive, no matter what city you live in. You can save hundreds of dollars a year if you plan ahead and give yourself time to get to work, play, or shopping by public transportation, a bike, or by foot.

If car costs are getting you down, don't worry. You may not be able to afford the Ferrari today, but you can own a model of one. Get yourself a toy car. Let it be a small dream, and know that as you cut your costs and pay your debts, you're that much closer to owning the real thing.

The Lazy Way

Getting Money on Your Side

	The Old Way	**The Lazy Way**
Taxi ride across town	$10	Bus ride $1.50
New car	$4,000 over dealer cost	$200 over dealer cost
Car won't run	$350 for bogus alternator you don't need	$45 for battery after you had the alternator checked
Auto insurance	Twice as expensive as need be	Only $75 a month! You called around.

Chapter
ten

Paying for Education Won't Leave You Penniless

Getting an education is meant to be one of the best times of your life. There's the thrill of intellectual discovery, the pleasure of thoughtful discourse, and, of course, all of those summer and spring breaks. It's just a bummer about the tuition thing. $14,565.82 for this year alone! Think of what you could do with that cash.

Joining the ranks of the erudite—or having your child evolve into someone more than a monosyllabic dust ball—doesn't have to leave you penniless. Of course, the earlier you start saving for college, the better. But even if you haven't planned ahead, there may be no better time to pay for an education.

In 1998, Uncle Sam began granting different tax write-offs for college loans and other assistance. Depending on the tax break, you may benefit whether you're an 18-year-old freshman or returning to college at 60.

The advent and widespread use of the Internet now means students can gain free and valuable information about scholarships, grants, and work-study opportunities with a click of a mouse or tap of the keyboard. Access to this "free money" may mean that going to an expensive private school could end up costing you less than attending a public university. There are ways to find out which schools can give you the biggest aid and grant packages before you enroll so you can gauge how much of a debt you'll face after you graduate.

Being a student doesn't mean being a financial hostage. There are many variable costs, from room and board to calling home, that can be significantly cut. College may not be the best, or cheapest, place to learn, either. There are other institutions where you can round out what you know, to brush up on your French, learn about personal finance, or sharpen other skills without paying hefty—or possibly any—tuition.

If you're already in debt or have defaulted on old school loans, there's hope for you, too. Loans can be temporarily deferred or consolidated so you can afford smaller payments. There are, of course, pros and cons to different payment options, but it's not difficult to find the best way for you to meet your obligations, save as much as you can, and have a financially bright future.

WHAT'S BEST FOR YOU IN THE LONG RUN?

The biggest mistake people make is assuming that they'll be penalized if they save for education. Too often, they believe that if they've saved $20,000 (or some other amount), they'll not qualify for scholarships or other financial aid.

This is a dangerous and flawed assumption. Families are not required to spend all their savings before they qualify for aid. On average, they must spend roughly six cents out of every dollar they have set aside in discretionary income for education expenses. Moreover, much financial aid now comes in the form of loans, not grants. The more money you have to pay off interest now to avoid taking out loans in the first place, the more debt you'll avoid, and the more you'll save in the long run.

Education IRAs: These new IRAs allow you to chip in up to $500 per year per student under age 18. The contributions are not tax deductible, but the gains in the account are. Withdrawals for education expenses also are tax free. An account must be shut down after 30 years. If it's never used by the intended child for education, the money can be spent to educate another family member.

YOU'RE WORKING OVERTIME TO SAVE FOR COLLEGE, BUT WHAT ABOUT JUNIOR?

Your budding Einstein may not be able to save much mowing lawns or baby-sitting, but there are things your genius can do to significantly cut college costs.

Obviously, the first step is to do well in school. There are scholarships based on need, but plenty of prizes and grants are given for merit. The better your child does in

YOU'LL THANK YOURSELF LATER

Put $1 in a jar every day. At the end of the month, deposit the cash in a learning account for yourself or your child. (It could be used for college, an educational trip abroad, vocational training, or other opportunities to expand your knowledge and sharpen your skills.) Keep depositing the dollars. If you do it from the time your child is born to when he or she is 17, you'll have set aside $6,205. If that money is put in an Education IRA, money-market fund, long-term certificate of deposit, or other interest-bearing account, it will be worth even more.

school, the more colleges will do to attract him or her and help pay for his or her tuition.

Have your student take courses in college he or she can take for free in high school. Many college freshmen skip entry courses by completing high school Advanced Placement classes.

Have your high school student enter competitions to earn college money and scholarships. There are prestigious awards, like the Westinghouse science award, the Coca-Cola Scholars Program, the College Fund/UNCF for 40 private African-American colleges and universities, America's Junior Miss Scholarship Program, and plenty of smaller ones, too.

Your guidance counselor can provide grant and scholarship information or log onto an Internet site for a quick listing of different aid sources:
www.yahoo.com/Education/Financial_Aid/Scholarship-Programs/

Get grants, scholarships, and other free money before you take out loans to pay for your education. Sources include local organizations such as churches and religious groups, the 4-H Club, Elks, the Chamber of Commerce, Kiwanis, and other community and civic groups often offer aid to area students.

Colleges and universities offer financial aid, and in general private schools tend to give out more money. When it comes time to look at campuses, ask about their scholarship programs and apply to schools that have generous aid packages.

YOU'LL THANK YOURSELF LATER

When family asks you what to get your son or daughter for Christmas, don't suggest a $25 sweater your child will outgrow or lose. Instead, set up an Education IRA and have them contribute what they can toward your child's college fund. A $25 birthday and Christmas check from Aunt Sarah may not seem a lot at first, but add the gifts up over 18 years, and you have $50 a year or $900 plus interest and tax-free growth.

If you're given a grant or scholarship package that doesn't cover your costs, you can appeal to obtain more. Chances are great that your scholarship was given to you based on your income, so introduce as much information about your financial predicament. Is your family caring for a sick child or aging parents? Did someone get fired from a job? Are your parents saving to send your three younger siblings to college, too? Hint, it's probably not a good idea to say you need the cash for your Saturday night poker game. Sit down and carefully explain why you think you deserve more.

LOG ONTO THE INTERNET TO GET GRANTS AND AID

There are literally hundreds of organizations offering aid, from large-scale corporations to private groups. The local library will have a list of grants and foundations. But the Internet may be the fastest, easiest source of one-stop shopping.

Check out Yahoo's list of financial aid:

www.yahoo.com/Education/Financial_Aid/Grants/

This site will get you in touch with everyone from the Carnegie Corporation of New York to GrantsNet (a link of funding for biological and medical sciences), the DeWitt Reader's Digest Fund, the National Science Foundation, the Paul and Daisy Soros Fellowships for New Americans (graduate school grants), or the Merrill Lynch Forum, which gives out $150,000 in grants to doctoral students who develop commercial products. The list has direct links to other grant information websites that have more information.

QUICK PAINLESS

Financial aid is awarded annually, so the great grant package you got this year could dry up next year. At the same time, college financial-aid officers are overworked and overwhelmed. You will find it a great help if your loan counselor knows who you are and cares about you. Always be polite, and send a quick thank-you note after you get your award or after they've spent three hours helping you apply for grants. This easy act of graciousness will clear the way when you need to reach them quickly in the future, or when you need extra assistance tracking down financial aid.

Your darlings are still in middle school, but you know it's going to be rough paying for their college. Start scanning lists of scholarship sources early. Are there grants for musical students? How about kids who want to major in French? Try to find sources of help that match your children's talents and interests, and tell them about the scholarships. This will be an added incentive for them to work harder and to see that they really can be rewarded for their efforts.

Fulbright Scholarships enable graduate students a year to study abroad by offering awards under the American Scholar program and the Visiting Scholar program. There is the Pre-Doctoral Fellowship and the Fulbright Teacher Exchange. To find out more, check out the Institute for International Education by writing or using their Internet site:

809 United Nations Plaza
New York, NY 10017
(212) 883-8200
www/iie.org

Write Your Own Grant Proposal and Get Money for Education

There are sources of grant information, but one of the best is The Foundation Center. The center has libraries across the country and offers an array of services, including grant-writing workshops so you can make sure your request for money is as compelling and eloquent as can be. The biggest centers are located in New York City, Atlanta, Cleveland, San Francisco, and Washington, D.C. Contact the main office in Manhattan.

79 Fifth Ave.
New York, NY 10003-3076
(212) 620-4230
www.fdncenter.org (with local addresses nationwide)

The government offers a variety of tuition breaks or assistance. You can quickly learn more about different grants by calling (800) 4-FED-AID, the Federal Student

Aid Information toll-free hotline. Grants you might want to know about include:

1. Pell Grants, which give up to $3,000 a year for four years. All colleges should have application forms for the federal grants.

2. Supplemental Education Opportunity Grants are given to the neediest students, but not all colleges offer them. Ask your college if they offer the grants. Award levels vary.

3. AmeriCorps education awards are given in exchange for community-service work. Students can work before, during, or after college and use the funds to pay off loans or tuition. Contact:

The Corporation for National and Community Service
1201 New York Ave. NW
Washington, DC 20525
(800) 942-2677
www.www.cns.gov/americorps/

The College Board, a nonprofit group of 3,000 schools dedicated to helping students and their bill-beleaguered parents make the transition to college, is a gold mine of information. Its excellent website has an SAT question of the day, information about college costs, loans, and a free scholarship search service.

The College Board
45 Columbus Ave.
New York, NY 10023
(212) 713-8000
www.collegeboard.org

IF YOU'RE SO
INCLINED

Businesses or labor unions often pay for employees' education, and some offer scholarships to children of their workers. Moreover, the Tax Relief Act of 1997 now allows workers to receive up to $5,250 a year toward undergraduate tuition that is tax free.

U.S. Armed Forces offers ROTC assistance, which is a merit-based scholarship program. Recipients get tuition, fees, books, and a monthly stipend. Call (800) USA-ROTC for information.

Veterans can obtain educational benefits from the Montgomery GI Bill, the Veterans Educational Assistance Program, or the Survivors' and Dependents' Educational Assistance Program.

Department of Veterans Affairs
810 Vermont Ave.
Washington, DC 20420
(800) 827-1000

The U.S. Department of Education has information about public education aid and federal loans. Check the Internet for easy-to-get information.

www.ed.gov/offices/OPE/Students/fedaid.html

WORK-STUDY PROGRAMS

It can be difficult to juggle studies with work. But working allows you to avoid loans and hefty debts. Most schools have federally funded work-study programs. Work-study jobs often enable students to work in areas of their study (for example, a Physics major gets work in the college science lab). As a result, a work-study job can be more interesting than flipping burgers.

Consider working off campus, where you can do everything from waiting tables to tutoring, cleaning houses, walking dogs, answering office phones, coaching youth sports leagues, or gardening. Many of these jobs are easy to schedule around your classes.

The more you pay for education today means the less you have to borrow, lower interest payments, and smaller debts in the future.

BORROW THE CHEAPEST LOANS FIRST

All loans are not created equal. There are tax breaks for some, and certain federal loans come with lower interest rates than commercial loans. In general, though, it's cheaper for students to borrow before their parents do. Remember that tax breaks are available to workers who don't earn much (like recent grads), which also may be another good reason for your student, not mom and dad, to borrow.

You can borrow money from private institutions or obtain *direct loans* from the government. Direct loans will cost the same to borrow. Schools receive loan funds directly from the federal government and then give them directly to students. Private loans come through banks.

Be sure to find out how often interest is calculated—the more often, the bigger your debt will be. Find out if your lender gives you options for repaying your loan (see below for more on repayment options). Payment flexibility may be important for you in the future depending on your income.

There are several different Federal loans for college students, but some offer lower interest rates than others:

IF YOU'RE SO INCLINED

Find someone who can teach you something for free. Want to learn how to knit or sew? Maybe your friend or the retiree who is bored out of her mind in the neighborhood retirement home would be glad to teach you in exchange for in-kind donations. Offer to do her weekly grocery shopping or read a book aloud to her for an hour a week. Consider posting a "want ad" for your teacher at the local synagogue or church, a senior center, or community room.

QUICK **n** PAINLESS

Teach yourself how to speak a new language without paying tuition. Language tapes are much cheaper than paying for classes. If you commute, use your 20 minutes sitting in traffic to conjugate verbs or to learn how to say "I love you" in Urdu.

■ Perkins Loans are federal loans for the nation's neediest students. They carry the lowest interest rates, now at 5 percent.

■ Subsidized Stafford Loans have interest rates between 6.86 percent up to 8.25 percent. The loans are made to needy students, but loan amounts are limited. Undergraduate college students can borrow up to $2,625 the first year, $3,500 the second year, and up to $5,500 while a student is in his or her third through fifth year of college.

The best part about subsidized Stafford Loans is that interest does not accrue while students are in school, and the first payment is not due until six months after graduation. (Everyone then assumes you'll have scraped yourself off the couch and will have found a job by then.)

■ Unsubsidized Stafford Loans are given to students who have too much income to qualify for subsidized loans. Students must pay interest while they are in school, which makes them more expensive than the subsidized Staffords.

■ Plus Loans are loans awarded to parents or guardians. The loan interest is limited to 9 percent, slightly higher than the Stafford Loans. If possible, try to have your student obtain the cheaper Stafford Loans before enrolling for a Plus Loan. There is no limit on loan amounts, but loans must be paid immediately.

NEW-AND-IMPROVED EDUCATION TAX BREAKS

Loan interest write-offs: Starting in 1998, interest paid during the first five years of a student loan is tax deductible. In 1998, maximum write-offs were $1,000. In 1999, the limit is $1,500, $2000 during 2000, and a maximum write-off will be $2,500 in 2001.

To qualify for the write-off, individuals must earn between $40,000 and $55,000, and couples' joint income should fall between $60,000 and $75,000.

Hope Scholarship Tax Credit: Families can claim $1,500 spent on each student as tax credit. The credit must be used during the student's first two years of college. So if you have a son and daughter in freshmen and sophomore year, you can deduct up to $3,000. The credit is given to individuals who earn no more than $50,000 or married couples earning up to $100,000.

Lifelong Learning Tax Credit: Families can get a tax credit of up to $1,000 per year for education costs spent on college juniors, seniors, graduate, or professional degree students. After the year 2002, the Lifelong Learning Tax Credit will increase to $2,000 a year. Unlike the Hope tax credit, the Lifelong credit does not have time limitations and is a great deal for older or graduate students.

THE PROS AND CONS OF CONSOLIDATING YOUR LOAN

If you've borrowed money from a variety of sources, it can be daunting to pay more than one check a month.

YOU'LL THANK YOURSELF LATER

Laws change, and sometimes to your advantage. Starting in 1998, Uncle Sam introduced new tax write-offs for college expenses. Keep up with current legislation that could save you cash. Pick up the phone and ask your tax consultant, experts like the folks at The College Board, or your financial aid counselor to find out if there are any new breaks or loopholes that give you bonuses, breaks, or other deals.

QUICK ● PAINLESS

Consolidation streamlines your loans. It also may be a way to reduce your monthly payment by stretching the loan out over time.

But be careful! Consolidating loans often costs you a lot more in the long run because you're taking a longer time to pay off your debt, so interest accrues faster.

To find out more about consolidation options, contact your school financial aid office, your lending institution, or:

U.S. Department of Education—Consolidation Department
P.O. Box 1723
Montgomery, AL 36102
(800) 557-7392 or TDD: (800) 557-7395

Consider the Alternatives

Standard payment plans require you to pay a fixed monthly payment—usually a minimum of $50—for up to 10 years. The length of the repayment period depends on the amount of the loan.

Extended payment plans allow borrowers to extend loan repayment 12 to 30 years on average. Watch out! The longer you pay your bill, the more you'll spend on interest in the long run.

Graduated repayment plans increase the cost of borrowers' payments over time. They're a good idea if you expect your income to increase. The interest rate payments will cost you more in the long run than if you stick to a standard repayment schedule.

DON'T LET TUITION TORTURE YOU—
TAKE CONTROL!

The average cost of tuition per year at a four-year public college is $3,111. Throw in books, room and board, phone calls home, and other expenses, and that bill jumps to $10,069. Four-year private college tuition is $13,664 per year, but add other costs, and the average price tag rises to $21,424.

To avoid the inflation bubble as much as possible, encourage your kids to use these 10 easy debt-cutting techniques to keep college costs under control:

1. Avoid credit cards. No offense, kids, but the damage you do with credit cards makes Helen of Troy look positively harmless. That's why your parents were hesitant about co-signing your card. Their fears are not unfounded. Interest rates and fees can accumulate very quickly if you're not paying your balances in full and on time. To avoid digging yourself into a massive hole, make sure you use your card only if you can pay your bill each month. And don't get caught paying for the dorm party with the card. If your buddies repay you in cash, there's a chance you'll spend it instead of using it to pay off the credit card.

2. Protect your phone card. You want to be nice and lend your phone card to a roommate. The next thing you know, someone has your access code. Don't share or reveal your card code, or you may wind up with unexpectedly high bills.

YOU'LL THANK YOURSELF LATER

Many lenders reward borrowers who pay their student loans off on time. Ask your lender if they offer similar breaks. Some of the best deals come from Washington-based Student Loan Marketing Association, known as Sallie Mae. Sallie Mae's Great Rewards program cuts interest rates by two whole points if the first 48 payments are made on time.

To find out more about the program, log onto the Internet: www.salliemae.com.

3. E-mail or (gasp!) write home! Calling home is expensive, but e-mail can be sent for the cost of a local call. Or why not write under a tree and enjoy the ambiance? It's very Jane Austen.

4. Call home on cheap, off-peak hours, which are usually on Sundays or late at night. (Your telephone carrier should tell you when rates dip.)

5. Buy second-hand textbooks. They'll be less expensive than new books. Make sure you get the correct edition!

6. Sell your textbooks—but only after your class ends. Then don't spend the money on beer. Set it aside for new books next semester.

7. Put yourself on an allowance. If you take out $20 from the ATM whenever you're broke, you'll spend more than if you limit yourself to a set allowance, say, $80 a week. Don't carry your bank card with you, or you may be tempted to withdraw money and make impulse purchases.

8. Don't borrow from or lend money to friends. Personal loans can strain or ruin relationships, and it's awful to owe someone money. It's also terrible when people don't pay you back.

9. Consider moving off campus. Room and meal plans may cost more than private rent and preparing your own food. Read classified rental ads, or contact an agency, to compare prices.

YOU'LL THANK YOURSELF LATER

Pay more than what you owe for your monthly student loan payment, or send in extra payments when you have a sudden financial windfall. Make sure any extra payments are credited to your principle, not the interest. You'll cut the time you spend paying off your college costs and save on interest.

10. Be a savvy shopper for household, school, and personal items. Stock up on inexpensive bulk goods like paper, pens, toilet paper, paper towels, and food staples if you live off campus. If you live on campus, keep an eye on what you spend for snacks, entertainment, and clothes.

HELP FOR THOSE OF YOU WHO HAVE DEFAULTED ON STUDENT LOANS, OR ARE ABOUT TO

One of the worst things you can do to sink your financial fate is to default on a student loan. If you fail to live up to your obligations, your credit report—which is used when you want to borrow in the future, buy or rent a house, or perhaps even get a job—will list very clearly that, educationally speaking, you're worse than a bonehead, you're a financial flake.

Lending institutions may seize tax rebates or your paycheck to get their money back. As they say in westerns, there are two ways to do this: go quietly and obey the law (and no one gets bothered), or get booted into line.

If you can't afford your monthly payment or you want to start repaying, contact your lender. You won't find a fleet of police cars with wailing sirens pull up to take you away if you reveal your whereabouts. Frankly, lenders will be happier to get some money from you than none at all, and you'll be greatly improving your chances of renegotiating a payment schedule that fits your budget. But remember that paying smaller amounts

will cost you more in interest in the long run, so try to pay off as much as you can.

Consider getting permission from your lender to defer payments or get a forbearance until you can afford to pay them. In case it slipped your mind, the difference between a forbearance and a deferment is as follows:

- Forbearance—You, the penniless but good-hearted, up-to-your-neck-in-loans graduate get permission from your lender to not make a payment for up to three months so you can catch up on you finances.

- Deferment—You, the penniless but good-hearted, up-to-your-neck-in-loans graduate get permission to stop paying loans while you're in the following circumstances:

1. Enrolled half-time in school (if the loan was made after July 1993) or enrolled full-time in school (if your loan was made prior to July 1993)

2. Work full-time in the Peace Corps or VISTA

3. Serve in the military

4. Are totally but temporarily disabled (physically, not mentally)

5. Are unable to work as a mother of young children

Get loan defaults off your credit report by rehabilitating them. If you pay 12 consecutive monthly payments on time for defaulted loans, the U.S. Department of Education will get your loan repurchased by a lending institution. Once the loan is rehabilitated, it will be taken out of default, and the credit bureau reports of the default will be deleted.

Getting Money on Your Side

	The Old Way	The Lazy Way
Buying textbooks	$35 for each new book	$20 for used books
Tuition	$10,069 on average	$7,069 with a Pell Grant that you don't have to repay
School taxes	No write-offs	As of 1998, tax laws give a variety of write-offs worth $1,000 to $2,500 annually per student

Health Costs That Won't Make You Sick

Your body works like a well-oiled machine. Your heart beats with the certainty and precision of a Swiss watch. Your legs are long and toned. Your healthy glow makes heads turn.

Then the alarm goes off, and you wake up to reality. The only thing that glows on your body is the perspiration as you heave up the stairs. Your heart goes into overdrive just walking around the block. And your legs. Well, Rubens would have loved them.

To be sure, striving for optimum health is a lofty and important goal. But getting motivated is difficult when staying healthy costs a lot of money. It's also depressing to face expensive fees for those items we'd rather avoid in the first place: increasingly thick eye glasses, root canals, or hospital stays.

There are ways to reduce many medical, health, and fitness costs, however. The most effective, and cheapest, method

for staying on top of your game is by staying on top of your game. Prevention, from embracing exercise to avoiding excesses, will cost you less in the long run than having to pay to get your health back.

The cost of the "unavoidables"—contact lenses and annual checkups—does not have to leave you seeing red and gasping for breath. Additionally, there are vital questions you can ask your doctor, insurance company, and other health-care providers before you check into the hospital or the examination room, so you won't check out with new debt to go with that new baby or new-and-improved body.

AN APPLE, A SIT-UP, AND PLENTY OF SLEEP KEEPS THE DOCTOR AWAY

It's a lot easier to stay healthy if you're in relatively good shape. And most common-sense health maintenance habits don't cost much, if anything at all. Here are a few basics to save your wallet, your sanity, and your physical well-being.

1. Get enough sleep. It costs you nothing, and you'll be able to accomplish far more (like paying the bills) when you're awake.

2. Eat a healthy diet. This does not have to be costly. In fact, chances are great that you'll save cash by not spending money on too many snacks or unhealthy food. Fresh veggies cost less than that double cheeseburger, too. (See chapter 7 for low-cost and delicious ways to feed yourself.)

3. Avoid health risks. Simple common-sense practices are free, and they'll keep you from paying huge medical and emergency bills.

- Don't use drugs or abuse alcohol.
- Don't drink and drive.
- Wear seatbelts.
- Keep poisons and pesticides in a safe place and away from children.
- Practice safe sex.
- Wear protective goggles when you operate machinery or other equipment.

4. Brush and floss those pearly whites. You'll not only have fresh breath and a killer smile, you'll be safe from the pain and agony of getting and paying for cavities.

5. Know basic first aid and keep a first aid kit so you can attend to minor scrapes and scratches without going to a doctor.

Must-Haves for the First Aid Kit:

- gauze bandage
- gauze pads
- bandages
- adhesive tape
- scissors
- cotton balls
- aspirin

QUICK ⬭ PAINLESS

Take a walk after dinner instead of sitting around feeling full. If you live in the country, pay attention to the stars overhead, or if you live in the city, notice the architecture. Your walk will be an adventure—not a chore— and a free way to improve your health.

- thermometer
- hydrogen peroxide
- calamine lotion
- antacid
- eye drops/wash
- petroleum jelly
- vitamin E tablets (good for blisters and burns)
- ice pack
- hot water bottle
- ace bandage

6. Stop smoking! This may not be the most effortless thing you've done, but at the very minimum you'll save roughly $2.50 a pack. That's $912.50 a year if you smoke a pack a day. Moreover, insurance costs more than twice as much for smokers than non-smokers. Extinguishing the habit can save you hundreds of dollars a year in health care alone, not to mention the wonders it will do for your health.

7. Exercise. You can do this for free, and yes, it can be fun. Some everyday ways to get in shape: Walk the dog, run, or dust off that old bike and go for a spin. Climb the stairs at work instead taking the elevator. Tone your triceps: rake leaves. Do a push-up (or two). Put on a great record and dance. Go sledding on a huge, snow-covered hill and make yourself walk up it at least 10 times. Instead of spending money at the mall, walk around it five times without stopping, and then let yourself make one

not-so-expensive purchase. It's a great way to reward your new, healthy body!

8. Sign up for or organize a sports team. It will be a free way to get in shape and a great opportunity to play with old or new friends.

9. Instead of joining a pricey health club, see if your local recreation department has free or low-cost passes to work out, do aerobics, swim, or play tennis.

10. If health clubs are your thing, make sure you get a good deal.

Health clubs cost roughly $40 to $60 a month, but there are ways to make sure you get the leanest bill possible.

▪ Join when no one else does. Everyone, including the family cat, goes on the traditional New Year's diet. As a result, clubs are jammed in January and less likely to offer price breaks. Gyms tend to be empty in the summer, when everyone is at the beach or hiding from swimsuits. This may be the best time to get a good deal.

▪ Try out the gym for free before you join. Ask for a guest pass to make sure you don't plunk down your hard-earned cash on a place you won't like.

▪ Ask the club to throw in extras if you join, such as free guest passes, free personal training sessions, a locker, or coupons for the juice bar.

▪ Don't join a club that has everything from indoor squash to yoga if you know you'll only use the weight room. You may be able to pay less to use just

QUICK ▪▪ PAINLESS

Suck in that tummy and squeeze in that ample bottom as you walk. Or put on your workout clothes and turn on the TV. Do sit-ups and push-ups when commercials come on television. You'll be the fittest couch potato around.

some of the equipment or join a bare-bones gym that has what you need and won't charge you for extras you don't use.

- Ask if the gym gives you discounts if you recruit others to join. Clubs often will knock off hefty fees ($100 in some cases) for each new member who you get to join. You could even get a group of friends and tell the club you'll all join if they give you a bargain rate. Many will be happy to take you up on the offer.

- If you can afford it, pay for a year's membership at once to get a discount rather than paying monthly dues. And don't forget to find out if your club pass may be used somewhere else.

- Ask your health-care provider if your insurance covers gym memberships. Many do. For example, U.S. Healthcare has a fitness reimbursement program. Prudential HealthCare has a program that lets you buy bike helmets for as little as $10 and has discounts on fitness equipment from golf clubs to athletic shoes.

CHECKUPS THAT WON'T DRAIN YOUR BANK ACCOUNT

Not that you want to feel like the family station wagon, but part of staying healthy involves checking in with the doctor on a regular schedule for tune-ups and checkups. And whether or not insurance is paying your tab—or you're digging into your own pocket—there are opportunities to obtain care without taking on huge bills.

YOU'LL THANK YOURSELF LATER

Not sure you can stick to your workout? Join a gym with a friend, spouse, family member, or someone else who will motivate you to keep going. Ask if you can get a break on health club fees if you join at the same time.

Get references and compare doctors' fees. Call ahead and find out what a doctor charges for office visits and other care before you step in the door. Make sure you ask about lab or other fees. Will you need to pay extra for X rays or blood samples? If so, how much will these be?

Use the local health department for free care. Local community agencies, and sometimes even civic groups like the Lions Club, often sponsor free cholesterol or breast-cancer screenings, back-to-school immunizations, and other medical services for free or at greatly reduced fees. Call your city or town health agency to find out if it or someone else has free medical programs. Don't forget to have your name put on mailing lists so you won't miss opportunities to save in the future.

Have a medical student give you a checkup before she or he increases prices. Medical schools often offer thorough checkups to the public for prices far lower than doctors. Med students perform the exams but are supervised by staff. At the University of California at Berkeley, for example, patients can get eye exams that include everything from vision to glaucoma tests.

MAIL-ORDER AND GENERIC MEDICINES, THE PRESCRIPTION FOR LOW-COST CARE

Generic brands are cheaper than name brands, so ask your doctor if the pills you take come in generic brands. While you're at it, see if it's possible to get a prescription for half the amount of pills with twice the dosage. Then split the medication in half. It's often less expensive to

YOU'LL THANK YOURSELF LATER

If you're overdue for a medical, eye, or dental exam, but you know you can't pay the full cost of a visit, set aside a little bit every month ($10 a month pays for an annual $120 check-up) or ask your doctor if you can pay monthly installments instead. This way you won't delay caring for your body. Putting off care can cost you a lot more to care for your health. Skeptical? Think about this. If you haven't had your teeth cleaned for years, chances are great that you'll have to pay to get rid of a mouthful of crater-sized cavities. (There's also the small bribe to the hygienist so she'll swear you've been flossing.)

buy 50 pills with twice the dosage than 100 tablets with half the medicinal power.

There are plenty of generic products you can purchase without a prescription, such as contact lens solution or aspirin. Shop at chain drugstores, like CVS, that may have lower prices than a private pharmacy. Remember, large chains like CVS have store-brand items that are as inexpensive as generic.

Shopping by mail has saved consumers billions of dollars. There are literally dozens and dozens of mail-order companies that can send you everything from birth control to sunglasses to generic and name-brand prescriptions. Check your local library or bookstore for mail-order books or search the Internet for vendors. You may want to consider the following resources, too.

Remember, if you buy through the mail, get a receipt to get reimbursement from your insurance company.

American Association of Retired Persons Pharmacy Service, for AARP members only: (800) 456-2277

Medi-Mail Pharmacy: (800) 922-3444

Cyber Pharmacy: (405) 485-2811 or
www.cyberpharmacy.com

MedExpress: (800) 808-8060 or
www.polypharmacy.com

Contact Lens Replacement Center: (800) 779-2654

You must have a current prescription, but I've found contacts at $100 less than the cost of ordering the lenses through an eye doctor.

ENSURING YOUR INSURANCE ISN'T TOO EXPENSIVE

If your employer or labor union pays for your insurance, you may not give much thought about how much it costs. But a whopping 41 million Americans are uninsured and have to buy their own—a daunting and potentially expensive endeavor.

There are ways to save, however, and it's fairly easy to make sure you have the coverage you need when you break a leg, have a baby, or need your eyes fitted for lenses.

Know how to navigate through the alphabet soup of health-insurance acronyms so you know what you're getting.

- Fee-for-service programs allow you to pay as you go. From a patient's point of view, this may be the most flexible in terms of choosing a physician or obtaining care.

- Managed-care programs ask you to pay a fixed amount for coverage. Depending on the program, you may face certain restrictions.

- Health Maintenance Organizations or "HMOs" are standard managed-care programs. Patients pay an annual premium to see doctors who are members of a network of care. Restrictions can be irksome. Many members have complained they don't get to choose their doctor or that the broadly defined category of specialized care isn't covered. Specialized care could be anything from going to the dermatologist to seeing a fertility clinic.

It's no fun shopping for insurance if you aren't covered by your employer or union. Don't despair. Invite providers to send you information, and take an afternoon to read through the different offers. Take notes. Who pays for prescriptions? Does anyone cover costs of gyms or counseling? How often can you get an eye exam? Reward yourself for this careful research by doing something that's fun.

The Lazy Way

■ Preferred Provider Organizations or "PPOs" are managed-care programs that also are made up of a network of doctors and hospitals. Patients have more flexibility in choosing their doctors than a standard HMO program and in getting specialized care. However, patients often must obtain permission from a primary care physician. (Primary care physicians are usually general practitioners who oversee a patient's care, see the patient first, and then decide whether or not to refer that patient to specialists for additional treatment.)

ANNUAL OR VARIABLE PREMIUMS

Patients pay an annual rate, usually in monthly installments, for coverage. Fees are usually lower for younger, presumably more healthy consumers—you know, people like the college kid guzzling beer and eating double-cheese pizza in front of the television.

With level premiums, patients pay a little more when they're younger so they can pay level rates as they get older.

Shop Around Before You Sign Up for Insurance

Your goal in obtaining insurance, of course, is to gain the most flexibility and access to the best doctors for the least amount of money and bureaucratic hassle. In other words, it's like being back in the fifth grade when you tried to bribe your little brother into taking over your dishwashing duties without handing over all of your allowance.

YOU'LL THANK YOURSELF LATER

Don't get pressured by hard-core sales tactics when you're buying medical insurance. If you don't understand what the sales rep is saying or you're not sure what something means ("what's a variable premium again?"), then ask. It's stupid not to clear up any questions you have or take the time to read the fine print. Remember, the best time to find out what you'll have covered is before you buy the insurance, not after your doctor's bill arrives in the mail.

In addition to asking about prices, finding out the following should help you trim costs, too:

- How much is the deductible (the amount you must pay before insurance pays the doctor)?

- What is the deductible for specialists or doctors who are not members of a particular managed-care network?

- Does the insurance pay for all or part of the cost of prescriptions, and are there any common prescriptions they don't pay for (like birth control or Viagra™)?

- Do people with pre-existing conditions have to pay more, or are they disqualified from coverage?

- Do people with particular jobs (writers, construction workers, belly dancers) have to pay higher premiums?

- How easy is it to change doctors?

- Do you need to see a primary care physician to obtain specialized care?

- How long does it take to get an appointment? (Don't take your insurance company's word for this! Call a few doctors you might be interested in seeing to find out how long you have to wait to get an initial appointment or if they're even taking new patients.)

- Who provides the care, a doctor or nurse?

- What types of medical care must be approved before you get treatment? (Transplant surgery often must be okayed ahead of time.)

- How many maintenance checkups do you get a year?

QUICK ⬤ PAINLESS

If you're choosing a plan where you have to see a primary care physician, make sure you won't be shut out in the cold waiting for care. Call a few doctors you'd be likely to choose as your primary care giver and ask to make an appointment as a new patient. If you have to wait a few months to get care, chances are you should pick someone else.

QUICK ● PAINLESS

When you're shopping for insurance, ask for discounts, or you may not get them! Does the insurance company give breaks to people who don't smoke, have low blood pressure or cholesterol readings, or who maintain healthy weights? Sometimes lower premiums for so-called preferred customers can save you hundreds of dollars a year.

- Are contacts and glasses covered?
- What "alternative" care is covered? (Some HMOs now pay for chiropractors and health clubs.)

USE HANDY QUOTE SOURCES TO GET THE BEST DEAL ON INSURANCE

It's easier than ever to compare insurance rates, especially with the Internet. Many companies have toll-free numbers, so your investigation doesn't have to cost a dime.

Here are just a few rate services you can find nationwide:

Wholesale Insurance Network (800) 808-5810

SelectQuote Insurance Services (800) 343-1985

MasterQuote of America (800) 337-5433

Quotesmith (800) 431-1147 or www.quotesmith.com

USAA (800) 531-8000

Disability Insurance

If you don't get disability coverage through work, you probably should buy an individual plan. Why? Think about it this way. What would you do if you knew you would not be able to work for months or even a year? How would you pay your bills? Think of how quickly that would get you into or exacerbate your already existing debt. That's why you need disability protection so you have some income. There is no rule to figure how much you should get, but choosing the amount of your coverage should be based on informed estimates of your expenses. (If you made a budget, you'll be in a better position to ascertain this amount.)

Life Insurance

If you have no dependents, it's probably a waste of money. If you do need life insurance, avoid a common and costly pitfall known as cash insurance.

Cash or Cash-Value Insurance are plans that include life insurance coverage plus guaranteed interest on any savings from your policy. But experts agree that you'll pay more for this investment-type of program. It's not worth it.

Term Insurance plans include life insurance coverage, and that's it. You can buy the coverage each year or through a level-premium plan where rates are curbed as you get older. All in all, term insurance is the most economical way to pay for life insurance.

COBRA (NO, WE'RE NOT TALKING SNAKES)

If you leave a job, you don't have to lose the umbrella offered by your employer's group health plan. COBRA plans allow you to keep receiving the insurance for up to 18 months after you leave. (You pay for this, of course.)

After 18 months, you can opt for a conversion policy, in which you purchase individual coverage from the same insurance carrier.

If your entrepreneurial heart is telling you to quit your 9-to-5 gig, COBRA and Conversion policies are a great opportunity to make sure you don't put yourself at risk of medical bills (which, after all, are hardly ever small) without the benefit of coverage.

IF YOU'RE SO
INCLINED

If you need to get glasses or contacts, ask your doctor about replacement insurance. For example, for a $25 annual fee, VSP Service (Tel: 800 615 1883) replaces lost or ripped contact lenses for far less than their original cost. However, you must have a current prescription.

MEDICARE AND MEDIGAP COVERAGE

Americans who are 65 or older qualify for the federal insurance known as Medicare. Medicare has a lot of gaps, however. So-called "approved charges" will be covered, but "excess charges"—for things like prescriptions, long-term care, or home health aides—are not covered.

Supplemental or "Medigap" insurance is a good way to close some of those potentially expensive gaps.

The American Association for Retired Persons—friends of anyone over 50—offers Medigap coverage:

AARP

601 E St. NW

Washington, DC (202) 434-2277

Additional reading:

The Complete Idiot's Guide to Buying Insurance and Annuities by Brian Breuel (Alpha Books) is a fabulous source on the ins and outs of all sorts of insurance.

HOSPITAL STAYS: MAKE SURE THEY DON'T TAKE MORE THAN JUST YOUR TONSILS

Going to the hospital is not like staying at a swanky hotel where your suite has a fully stocked minibar. Without thinking, you open a few of those tiny bottles of gin, gulp down the can of macadamia nuts, and then wonder about room service. Only later do you discover you'll be charged for these "free" bar items at 10 times the cost of buying them at the store.

A hospital room may not have a bell boy, but you should be aware that the ice pack, that gown that never closes in the back, the baby diapers, and telephone may be medical science's answer to the hotel minibar. These apparently free items have been known to find their way onto hospital bills. Before you use anything, ask if you'll be charged. It may even be easier to bring your own pajamas.

Other Ways to Avoid Huge Hospital and Medical Costs

1. Call your doctor instead of going in for a visit. A phone consultation may cost you less than seeing your doctor in person.

2. Find out what fees for treatment cost before you get help.

3. Keep receipts for all medical bills, especially if you have a co-payment and will be getting reimbursed from insurance.

4. Check and verify all bills to make sure you're not getting double-billed or charged for lab tests or other treatment you never received.

5. Don't get a private hospital room. They cost a lot more than a shared room. Besides, wouldn't it be nice to commiserate with a new pal?

6. If you're scheduling a hospital stay, find out if it's cheaper to go in the middle of the week or avoid holidays when rooms may cost more. (See, it really is like Holiday Inn.)

There's no such thing as an inexpensive hospital bill. So if you're laid up for some time, try to avoid pitfalls, but don't make yourself ill with worry. Use your time at the hospital to rest. The bills will be there when you're discharged so you might as well treat yourself kindly while you recouperate.

The Lazy Way

Getting Money on Your Side

	The Old Way	The Lazy Way
Replace contact lens	$250 per lens	$175 with replacement insurance
Prescription filled	$23 for name-brand	$12 for generic
Joining a health club	$50 per month if you join Jan. 1, plus a $100 intro fee	No fee and $42 a month if you join in the summer when the gym is empty

You Don't Have to Pay (Lots) to Play: Have Fun Without Getting a Financial Hangover

You know that diet you keep trying, the one where you don't get to eat anything besides carrots and skim milk? You don't stick to it because there's nothing tasty. Financial diets will be a bust, too, if you don't let yourself have any fun. Just because you're watching your wallet doesn't mean you can't watch a movie, read a good book, enjoy pretty flowers in your garden, or have other so-called luxuries. You just have to know how to have fun without spending so much. (Look at Cinderella—hardly a wardrobe to speak of but she went to the ball.) It's time to be your own fairy god-mother and kick up your heels.

Bargains are the stuff of fairy tales. In fact, there are plenty of obvious ways to save. Swap books with pals, buy discount tickets to the theater, or borrow, instead of buy, the latest Stephen King thriller. There are also other ways to keep expenses in check if you're creative and know where to dig for bargains.

Once again, the Internet is a great source to track down discount stores for everything from inexpensive books to arts and crafts supplies. Can't afford a fabulous tour of Asia this year? Then how about looking for lectures on Tibetan art at the local library or take a walking tour through your own home town. Want an English garden just like those you find in slick home and entertainment magazines? You don't need to hire a pricey gardener. Buy flats of discount flowers and split the cost with friends, or use recycled materials for supplies. And yes, you can go see plays or musical concerts for free.

There is no limit to the fun you can have if you're willing to look for bargains or create your own. So, don't mope. Being a little strapped for cash doesn't mean you can't have fun. Just ask Cinderella.

Let Them Entertain You Without Gouging You

Movies:

Depending on where you live, a two-hour movie costs $9 a ticket, and that's before you visit the concession stand. It doesn't have to be so much to ogle Mel Gibson or Cameron Diaz.

- Go to matinee shows. Many theaters have bargain afternoon shows for about one-third the cost. And chances are the theater will be less crowded so all you shorties don't have to get stuck behind the local basketball star.

- Look at Golden Oldies and Funky Art Flicks. Old movie houses, the ones that sell really good cappuccino and baked goods, often run old classics and charge just a fraction of the cost. Old movie houses often are listed in the movie section of your newspaper or in local entertainment magazines that cater to a particular city, such as *Time Out* in New York or the *Bay Area Guardian* in San Francisco.

- What are they playing at the museum or college? Universities and museums often have movie festivals that are open to the public and are either free or a nominal fee to get in. Plus, how often do you get to see the silver screen among great paintings or ivy-covered towers? Pick up a calendar of events from your local school or museum to see if there's anything worth watching.

- Rent a movie or swap with friends if they have a video collection.

Books:

- Love your library! Where else can you get books, magazines, musical recordings, books on tape (for those boring commutes), and even movies for free? Libraries often have book sales. Dig around, and you may leave with a bag of paperbacks for just a few dollars. Remember to return everything you borrow on time so others may enjoy, too!

QUICK 🔘 PAINLESS

Become an usher. There's nothing like sitting in a concert hall as a full orchestra launches into a symphony. But sometimes tickets can cost a bit too much for many of us. Ushering is a great way to hear music for free. Call your local concert hall and ask to speak to the person who runs the ushering program to see if they accept volunteers.

- Swap those books (or music). This is when you care about what's between your friends' covers...book covers, that is. Have a little party, serve cookies and tea (or pretzels and beer), and ask everyone to bring a bag of books they don't want anymore. Swap, and expand your reading collection for free! If you want new music, have a CD swap.

- Shop at secondhand bookstores. You might not find the book you want, but chances are you'll find something to read without paying full cover cost.

- Check out Amazon.com. This online mail-order service has taken everyone by storm. You can enjoy discounts on all books, and you'll get your books delivered to your door within a day or two: www.amazon.com.

  You can call (206) 346-2992 or write Amazon at 549 S. Dawson, Seattle, WA 98108.

Art and Architecture:

- Go to museums for art and more. Many museums are free, but some may also charge hefty fees. Always ask if you can qualify for senior, group, or student discounts. Find out when museums have "free" nights and mark your calendar. Museums also have other freebie perks like jazz concerts, films, guided tours, children's art programs, and lectures. Find out and take advantage of all of their services.

- Take or go on your own walking tour. Look for local tours advertised in your community paper or take yourself on a walk through a historic district in your city. It's free and a fun way to enjoy some great architecture or learn about local history. Or, if you live in the country, bicycle past Colonial farm houses or country villas. Take a picnic basket and make it an appetizing adventure.

■ Have an art day at home. You don't need to have kids to do this, but it's a great way to keep them entertained, too. Use leftovers—from old paint to fabric, egg containers, buttons, and so on—and make your own art. You may even start a quilt or end up making holiday gifts. If you need art supplies, many mail-order companies have discount materials. Consider some of the following sources:

Art Express
Dept. C
P.O. Box 21662
Columbia, SC 29212
(800) 535-5908

The Art Express catalog costs $3.50, and there's a $25 minimum order, but you can get up to 40 percent off paint paper, canvases, easels, and more.

Cheap Joe's Art Stuff
374 Indian Park Rd.
Boone, NC 28607
(800) 227-2788

The catalog is free, and you can find prices slashed 30 to 60 percent for paper, paint, art books, and other supplies. There are no shipping costs for brushes!

Don't throw out those wilted roses! Dry them and use the petals for homemade potpourri or put them in your drawer to keep your clothes smelling fresh.

The Lazy Way

Music:

- Support local music groups. You don't have to go to Carnegie Hall or an Eric Clapton concert to hear great music. You can find great classical music in churches or synagogues, or even at the local community center, or at most college campuses. Likewise, drop in for a noontime jazz concert at a local school or museum. Use your community or arts paper to find out where you can hear music without paying hefty ticket or cover charges.

- Play Your Own Tune. If you really love music, why not sharpen your rusty piano skills or learn to play the guitar? Join a band or play by yourself. You can offer to swap services (walk a dog, give a car a tune-up, or make dinners) for music lessons.

Pet Care Options

Cats and dogs can be our best friends, but they sure know how to eat us out of house and home. The good thing about pets, however, is that you don't have to shop at Tiffany's to spoil them. Here are just a couple of things that will save you a bundle of money in the long run:

- Ask your veterinarian if it would be healthy to put your dog or cat on a menu of dried pet food. Wet food is much more expensive and sometimes contains lots of fats that aren't healthy for your precious pet. You may also want to ask your veterinarian to recommend lower cost pet food, including generic brands sold by supermarket chains.

- Use discount mail-order goods, like Discount Master Animal Care, One Maplewood Drive, Hazleton, PA 18201, (800) 346-1749 or R.C. Steel Co., Dept. WC, P.O. Box 910, Brockport, NY 14420-0910, (800) 872-3773.

Garden:

- Buy plants at the end of seasons. A flat of pansies may cost you far less if you wait until late spring, yet it also may give your garden a special spark if you take care to keep the flowers alive. End-of-summer is a great time to buy perennial plants from nurseries at discounted prices.

- Buy in bulk. It's often less expensive to buy flats of flowers instead of individual plants. If you don't need many, shop and share the cost with a friend.

- Use old wood broom and mop handles for vegetable stays instead of buying posts.

- Use a mixture of white vinegar and water to repel flies instead of buying costly insecticides.

- Save "starter" pots when you buy young plants and use them to cultivate flowers from seeds. Seeds are less expensive and can be started at home in the winter. You'll have plenty of flowers by the time spring breaks.

- Join a community garden. If you don't have a yard but want to grow your own vegetables and flowers, call your local recreation center or garden supply store to see if there are community gardens you can join. Or satisfy your green thumb cravings and give a

IF YOU'RE SO
INCLINED

How about a plant swap! You can swap plants with your friends and neighbors. You can post it in the paper and get yourself some beautiful new plants—free of charge!

Did you grow too many tomatoes? Make sauce and freeze it. Turn fruit into jam. You can savor fresh home-made tastes all year round or give the jam, sauces, zucchini bread, etc. as inexpensive but thoughtful gifts.

little by volunteering for organizations that plant gardens in the city. Green Guerillas in New York City transforms abandoned lots into colorful, peaceful havens for the young and old to enjoy. It costs nothing to volunteer, and the satisfaction from volunteering and learning how to keep those rose bushes alive is priceless.

- Water at night and cut down on water bills. Watering in the day is less efficient.

- Use plants that are indigenous to your area. An orchid will be very expensive if you live in Vermont. Inquire about the plants that grow naturally in your area and grow those. They'll be less expensive to buy.

- Use cuttings to get more flowers. Need more ivy? Clip a little, put it in water, and have it grow roots so you can plant more.

- Start a compost pile. Don't dump your lawn clippings, dried leaves, orange peels, or coffee grinds. Make a compost pile and grow your own rich fertilizer.

Computers:

Get free training. If you know nothing about computers, it's probably a good idea to take a class before you buy one of your own. Acquiring computer skills also isn't a bad idea if you want to beef up your resume, too. Classes can be expensive, so keep some of these options in mind:

- Visit the library. Libraries are adding technology to their collections of books and periodicals. And librarians are some of the best teachers in the world.

Go to your library and see if it has a computer with Internet access (many do). Ask your librarian to show you how to log onto the Internet. Need a website to visit? Pick one of the addresses in this book for sources of information on saving mortgage costs, finding low-cost clothes, or more. (Hint, Web addresses are those that start with the following tag: www....)

- Go to computer training schools. Open any phone book, and chances are you'll find dozens of listings for computer training schools. Don't have a phone book? Check out classified ads in your paper or in weekly publications, such as the *Village Voice*. Call and compare prices. Does the class fee cover extra training sessions? If you sign up for a second class, can you get a discount? Don't just enroll in the first school you find.

- Get work to train you. It never hurts to ask your boss if your company will pay to have you hone your skills. Make sure that you have carefully thought out reasons why you need to learn more computer skills before you ask your company to pay for you to learn more about that machine on your desk.

- Write off the computer training. Keep any receipts for computers or training you may pay for and see if you can deduct your expenses from taxes at the end of the year.

- Buy computers by mail. When you know what you want, it may be cheaper to buy what you need—from a new terminal to a modem—directly from

YOU'LL THANK YOURSELF LATER

Don't spend a fortune on paper. Use paper that's gone through the computer printer as notepaper for grocery lists, notes to your family, or somewhere to jot down the first sentence to your great American novel.

manufacturers. Computer publications are filled with advertisements for a plethora of products. You can usually find a laptop or personal computer for less money than going to the neighborhood store.

■ Consider buying a secondhand computer. Scan newspaper classified ads for secondhand computers. Some stores allow people to post ads on bulletin boards. Or call stores directly and ask them if they deal in used computers. Beware, a used computer probably won't have a warranty, so make sure you're not buying a dud.

Getting Money on Your Side

	The Old Way	**The Lazy Way**
Feeding Fido	$14 for a bag of rawhide chews	$4 for an entire box of rawhide you get through a discount mail-order supplier
Going to the movies	$9 for a ticket for latest blockbuster	Half-priced tickets for matinees or reruns of old classics. Borrow movie videos for free from the library.
Music	Wait in line for overpriced concert tickets	See and hear live music for free by ushering

The Final Frontier: Saving for Emergencies, Rainy Days, and a Golden Future

You'd be a lot happier if everyone would stop talking about retirement funds, investments, and saving. You're too busy fretting about bills to worry about what comes next. It's depressing.

Cheer up. And then pay attention to all that talk you'd rather not hear. It's a terrible mistake not to plan ahead or to invest in yourself.

Traditional safety nets are growing threadbare. More than one politician has warned that there won't be enough Social Security—the nation's retirement and disability benefits program—to support our aging baby boomers. Moreover, Social Security isn't adequate income for those who receive it now. Retirees today receive benefits that are worth 40 percent of what they used to earn as wage earners. Unless you're billionaire/financier George Soros, 40 percent of your paycheck won't be enough for you, either. How about pension plans? If you have one, consider yourself lucky. Half of America's 120 million employees don't.

To be sure, many of our fiscal futures are a little more than tenuous. Yet for some reason, we aren't jolted into saving. That's mind boggling. If we get caught in the rain, we seek shelter. If we're hungry, we eat. Yet two-thirds of America's households—a whopping 65 million—won't be able to meet one or more major goals because they don't have any financial plan for the future. The average retirement savings account is worth $10,000.

HOW LONG COULD YOU LIVE ON $10,000?

There is good news amid the bad. Elimination of debt is the most important step you can take toward having a promising financial future. If you've been trimming expenses, you're well on your way to being prepared. Give yourself a big hug.

Time also is a huge, but free, source of wealth. It allows compound interest to grow at accelerated rates and turn modest savings into handsome windfalls. Consider this. A young person who invests $2,000 a year from age 22 to 30—or $18,000 total—will have more than $579,000 by the time he or she is 65 provided that this money earns 9 percent interest.

Compare that $579,000 nest egg to a $470,000 savings. That's how much you would have if you invest

You're starting to set money aside for your future. Reward yourself by getting yourself a piggy bank, a stuffed pig Beanie Baby, or something to remind you of your accomplishment!

The Lazy Way

$2,000 a year from the time you're 30 to 65. In other words, you would put aside $70,000—far greater than the $18,000 when you're in your twenties—but the 9 percent interest would have less time to do its magic, so you get far less for your money.

Where do you begin once you decide to save and invest? There are no specific, foolproof answers. If there were, we'd all be living in beach-front villas and sipping bottles of champagne. Nevertheless, you should know the difference between stocks, mutual funds, Roth IRAs, and traditional IRAs, and other investment options. Once you have knowledge, you can micro-manage your own accounts or know enough to hire savvy, reliable financial experts to help plan a comfortable future, invest wisely, save for big emergencies, build toward long-term goals, or prepare for a distant rainy day.

SAVING FOR THE FUTURE WHEN YOU'RE NOT SURE HOW MUCH YOU'LL NEED FOR EMERGENCIES

If you're saving for emergencies, many experts advise you to set aside three to six months worth of income. That should be sufficient in case you're between jobs. That week's worth of grocery money stashed in your linen closet, however, is not adequate.

If you do find yourself faced with costly emergencies, try to avoid getting mired in debt. Use your credit card only as a last resort. If you need cash, consider the following sources:

YOU'LL THANK YOURSELF LATER

Some have paid for emergencies by obtaining loans that are tied to their assets. This could be as simple as a money market account or certificate of deposit. But be extremely careful about mortgage-backed home-equity loans. There are blizzards of radio, television, and print ads extolling the virtues of putting your home up as collateral, but the last thing you want to do if you're in an emergency is hock your home. It jeopardizes the roof over your head, and you'll rarely get a fair loan based on the bank's assessment of your property.

The 3 Worst Things to Do When Saving for Emergencies:

1. Take any cash in your checking account and go on vacation.

2. Use the money in your emergency fund to throw a really great party.

3. Hire a fortune teller to tell you when you'll have emergencies. If she says you're safe, use your emergency fund on something fun instead.

Overdraft bank loans. Overdraft protection will keep you from bouncing a check, and you'll be able to repay the bank in case you spend more than you have. Keep in mind that banks don't have to give you this protection, so if you've been bouncing checks like rubber balls, you may have to rebuild your credibility before you earn this service.

"Just in case" lines of credit. So-called "signature loans" are approved by the bank and ready for you to cash in when and if you have an emergency. Again, you probably will need solid credit to obtain a signature loan. (So consider this yet another reason for getting rid of your debts.)

SAVING FOR THE FUTURE WHEN YOU'RE NOT SURE HOW MUCH YOU'LL NEED FOR RETIREMENT

Retirement goals are a little more difficult to set than emergency funds, but it's not impossible. The American Savings Education Council, part of the nonprofit group Employee Benefit Research Institute in Washington, D.C., has developed the following, easy-to-use "Ballpark Estimate" formula to help you figure out how much you have to save to have a comfy retirement.

The Savings Council assumes that you'll need at least 70 percent of your current salary to maintain your standard of living minus certain assets. Fill out the following Ballpark Estimate worksheet or check out an online interactive version on the ASEC website (www.asec.org)

to see exactly how much you should set aside per year until you finally call it quits and head into the sunset with that snazzy pocket watch.

1. Enter 70 percent of your current income here: _____
   (To figure this out, multiply your income by .7)

2. Enter:

Social Security (If you earn less than $25,000, enter $8,000. If you earn between $25,000 and $40,000, enter $12,000. If you earn more than $40,000, enter $14,500)

_____

Pension, if any, from employer.   _____
Part-time income.   _____
Other (IRA, inheritance, and so on)   _____
   Total value of Part 2 (add them up)   _____

3. Subtract total from 2 from Line 1.   _____

This is what you'll need to earn for each of your retirement years to maintain your current standard of living. Don't gasp. You can do it. Go to step 4.

4. Multiply amount from Line 3 with the following:

I will retire at 55 (multiply by 21)
I will retire at 60 (multiply by 18.9)
I will retire at 65 (multiply by 16.4)
I will retire at 70 (multiply by 13.6)

_____

5a. I don't expect to retire before age 65.
    Go to line 6.

I will retire before 65. Multiply your Social Security benefit in section 2 with the following:

It's important to remember that you can't get out of a financial emergency by borrowing money, and any loan must be repaid with interest. Build an emergency fund into your personal budget until you have saved adequate cushioning (again, a nest egg worth three to six months earnings) for life's lumps and bumps.

IF YOU'RE SO
INCLINED

It can be difficult planning your retirement if you have no idea how much Social Security you'll get. The Social Security Administration can get your personal earnings and benefit estimate directly online or by mail. Contact the SSA weekdays at (800) 772-1213 or write the SSA, Office of Public Inquiries, 6401 Security Blvd. Room 4-C-5 Annex, Baltimore, MD 21235 or via the Internet: www.ssa.gov.

I will retire by 55 (multiply Social Security by 8.8)

I will retire by 60 (multiply Social Security by 4.7)

_____

5b. Add Lines 4 and 5. Enter here: _____

6. Multiply your savings to date, including a 401(k), IRA, Keogh, or other retirement plan by the following factors:

I will retire in 10 years. (Multiply savings by 1.3)

I will retire in 15 years. (Multiply savings by 1.6)

I will retire in 20 years. (Multiply savings by 1.8)

I will retire in 25 years. (Multiply savings by 2.1)

I will retire in 30 years. (Multiply savings by 2.4)

I will retire in 35 years. (Multiply savings by 2.8)

I will retire in 40 years. (Multiply savings by 3.3)

_____

7a. Subtract Line 6 from total of Line 5b _____

This is the savings you'll need by retirement.

7b. To get this amount, I need to save this much each year.

I want to retire in 10 years. (Multiply $ amount on Line 7 by .085)

I want to retire in 15 years. (Multiply $ amount on Line 7 by .052)

I want to retire in 20 years. (Multiply $ amount on Line 7 by .036)

I want to retire in 25 years. (Multiply $ amount on Line 7 by .027)

I want to retire in 30 years. (Multiply $ amount on Line 7 by .020)

I want to retire in 35 years. (Multiply $ amount on Line 7 by .016)

I want to retire in 40 years. (Multiply $ amount on Line 7 by .013)

Enter result of Line 7. This is the amount you need to save each year for retirement.

_____

In addition to the ballpark estimate, the American Savings Education Council website has great information on financial planning and savings. Log on or write them for copies of their brochures.

American Savings Education Council
c/o Employee Benefit Research Institute
2121 K St. NW — Suite 600
Washington, DC 20037-1896
www.asec.org

GETTING FROM HERE (WITH $2.57 IN YOUR POCKET) TO THERE (WHEN YOU HAVE $257,000 IN YOUR NEST EGG)

1. Get rid of your debt.

2. Save for the future by making sure you have a diverse portfolio of investments.

3. Take advantage of employer-savings programs such as a 401(k).

4. Consider getting financial advice.

Congratulations! You figured out what you need to save each year to have enough for retirement. You're now part of an exclusive minority. Only one in four Americans knows what he must set aside for life after work. Congratulate yourself with a treat, and by all means, tell your parents. They'll be pleased to know you've learned something more than baseball statistics and the lyrics to Pink Floyd's *The Wall.*

It may seem impossible to save when you're trimming expenses, but think how strapped for cash you'll feel when you're retired and have no savings. Set aside something from your paycheck for your future. You'll soon learn to pay yourself first, and you'll see you can get buy without the cash you've put aside for your future.

You've made an effort to eliminate most of your debts. But what does it mean to have diverse investments? Why is a 401(k) so important? You can't invest your money wisely or hire the best experts if you don't know what you're talking about.

The following list includes easy-to-understand definitions for more common investment strategies. Keep in mind this is just a start. Nothing beats a more thorough education about finances (and we'll talk about this some more in a bit). For now, review the list and see how much you know and don't know.

MUST-KNOW INVESTMENT LINGO

Retirement Funds

- *Annuity.* (See under Fixed Income Investments.)

- *401(k).* Virtually all financial experts advise people to take advantage of 401(k) plans because they are literally gifts of money that make your fund grow without effort. The perk is that your employer contributes a percentage and sometimes matches every dollar you set aside, which means you get a lot more for your money.

- *Individual Retirement Account or IRA.* A retirement plan in which individuals can set aside as much as $2,000 a year, and working couples can set aside $4,000 while deducting these contributions from their income taxes. You must pay tax when you withdraw money from your IRA. Similarly, you cannot take money from IRAs until you are 59 $\frac{1}{2}$, unless it is for a first-time home purchase or for college education. If you do make an early withdrawal, you'll pay penalty fees.

- *Roth IRA.* As of 1998, individuals are allowed to invest up to $2,000 a year into a Roth IRA. Unlike the traditional IRA, contributions in a Roth are not tax deductible, but withdrawals will be tax free upon retirement. That could mean big savings—especially since compound interest will make your Roth IRA worth more than your total contributions.

- *Keogh Plan.* A retirement plan much like a 401(k) for self-employed workers. Contributions to your Keogh are tax free, but you pay income tax on withdrawals.

Fixed Income Investments

- *Annuity.* An investment retirement account backed by insurance companies, which pays you fixed payments for life or for a certain period of time after you reach age 59 $^{1}/_{2}$. Annuities earn higher interest than traditional savings accounts, and earnings are tax free until you withdraw funds, at which point you pay regular income tax. Unlike an IRA, deposits to your annuity cannot be deducted from taxes. If you die before you collect your annuity, the fund can be left to a beneficiary of your choice.

- *Bonds.* Bonds are the plain-looking person at the ball. They're not very glamorous or sexy, but some of them should be asked to dance if you don't want to get your financial toes trampled.

QUICK PAINLESS

Financial jargon tripping you up? Feeling stupid about investments. Read one article a day from the business section of your local paper. You'll be surprised how much you'll learn with little effort. Or log onto financial web sites. Many have great glossaries so you can find out the meaning of an IPO, an American Depository Receipt, or a coupon bond in just a few clicks of your keyboard. Need a few good web sites? Check out www.smartmoney.com; www.cnnfn.com; and www.asec.org/terms.htm. (that's the American Savings Education council) to get a good start.

In essence, bonds are nothing more than certificates of debt (when you buy bonds, you're essentially lending money) that pay you a fixed amount of money over time plus interest, which is called yield. The length of time it takes to repay a bond is called a length of maturity.

There are corporate, state, federal (called Treasuries), and municipal (tax-free) bonds.

You may purchase bonds individually, or you can buy mutual funds that are made up of a collection of bonds.

Bonds are rated according to how risky they are as investments. A superlative rating of AAA is considered a super-safe investment, while a BBB- is low.

Generally, yields rise if bonds are risky (you get paid more for lending money to an institution with shakier credit). Yields also are generally higher for bonds that have longer lengths of maturity, the time it takes to be fully paid. When bond prices drop, yields rise. Bond yields reflect the state of the economy and rise and fall following the interest rates.

■ *Certificates of Deposit.* These are the CDs that don't make music. Sold by banks, they are short-term debt you fund in turn for interest that usually is higher than a traditional savings account. A CD's rate of maturity can be a short period of time, say three months, or longer, such as five years. The longer the rate of maturity, the more interest you'll be paid. CD's are safe, guaranteed investments, but as a result you'll earn less than if you put money in something riskier like stocks.

- *Treasuries.* These are bonds sold by the federal government. A Treasury Bill is a debt that will be repaid to the investor within a year. A Treasury Note will have a 2-year, 5-year, or 10-year rate of maturity. Treasury Bonds are paid off after 10 years.

- *Money Market Fund.* A mutual fund that buys "money" such as CDs and Treasury Bills, which can be sold within a 24-hour period, which means it's "liquid" or easily transferable into paper money. Money market funds tend to be good, safe bets for parking money until you have a better place or enough to invest it elsewhere.

Equities and More

- *Stocks.* Stocks, called equities, are the pretty girl (or handsome guy) at the ball. They can make your heart soar, or break, as the nature of stocks is to fluctuate. The trick is choosing the ones you want to spend a very long time with.

  When you buy "shares" of stocks, you own part of a company. Stock earnings rise and fall for a variety of reasons that affect earnings of a company. As a result, stocks can offer great profits on your investment, but because returns are tied to unpredictable factors, such as earnings, they are riskier investments. If you have time to let your money grow, stocks are well worth buying provided you get advice and research your investment. Some stocks

Get help investing in your future. When your Aunt Martha or mom and dad ask what you want for Christmas or your birthday, control the urge for a new outfit or a gift certificate to the mall. Ask for a better deal: a certificate of deposit, money put into your IRA, or a small donation for your retirement fund. It's the kind of practical gift they'll be pleased to give.

The Lazy Way

pay dividends, or shares that are automatic reinvestments in the company. Other "no-yield" stocks don't pay dividends because they use profits to reinvest back into the company.

Quick and Easy Information on Stocks:

The Standard & Poor's Bond Guide and Stock Guide
www.standardpoor.com
ValueLine (tracks stocks and mutual funds)
(800) 223-0818

Mutual Fund. A mutual fund is a collection of stocks and/or bonds that are sold as a group to different investors who have pooled their money together. (In other words, they're the TV dinners of Wall Street. They come with meat, potatoes, beans, and a piece of cake. You buy them because you don't want to buy and prepare individual courses.)

When you invest in a fund, you get a complete serving made up of stocks and/or bonds. Thus, a mutual fund is different than going out and buying individual shares of Exxon or General Electric.

To stick with the dinner analogy…You can buy vegetarian TV dinners, Tex-Mex, or plain ol' Salisbury steak and potatoes. Mutual funds specialize in all fields of investments: energy, technology, aggressive growth, balanced funds, global, health, medical, small cap (made up of smaller companies), or even index funds like the Standard & Poor's 500.

The beauty of mutual funds is that for a reasonable amount of money, you may automatically invest in a diverse collection of investments without having to pay a great deal more to buy or sell "odd lots," which are fewer than 100 shares of stock.

The other advantage to mutual funds for the inexperienced investor is that they are run by mangers who are paid lots of money for their expertise in choosing which stocks go into their funds and which ones don't cut it. However, be aware that a manager can blow it, too. Do background checks on funds.

You can find out about a fund's performance by reading the so-called Morningstar report, available at most libraries or on the Internet: http://morningstar.net.

Even if you don't choose to buy into the S&P 500 Index, try to invest on a regular schedule, say four times a year. This way, you'll ride out the highs and lows on the market, and your investment will continue to grow.

NOW THAT YOU KNOW WHERE YOU CAN PUT YOUR MONEY, HOW DO YOU CHOOSE WHAT'S BEST FOR YOU?

Knowing how to invest and save for your future is like going on a California vacation when you live in Vermont. There are many routes you can take. You may choose country roads, superhighways, or even fly to get to the state of earthquakes and Disneyland. But beyond those choices, you know there are certain common-sense rules to follow, like heading west.

A COMPLETE WASTE OF TIME

The 3 Worst Things to Do When Buying Stocks:

1. Buy no-load mutual funds—you're not going to have to pay any fees. (No-load funds may have management fees that could cost you as much as a "load" stock.)

2. Buy stocks based on a tip you got from your buddy at the local bar. Who needs the experts?

3. Wait until you're ready to invest in your future. Even if it takes years!

You don't have to be a millionaire to own a bit of America's biggest, boldest, and most successful companies. The Standard & Poor's 500 Index mutual fund is made up of 500 stocks such as AT&T, Coca-Cola, and General Motors, and the index has been used as a common barometer of the stock market because it is so big. You can spend as little as $500 to have your IRA invested in S&P 500 stocks or $1,000 to invest in the index without it being tied to any retirement fund. Additionally, the index is a "no-load" fund, and you don't have other fees, either, provided that you don't sell within 90 days.

You may choose among different investment opportunities, but your decision should depend on your needs and general guiding principles. Think about the following questions. Your answers will guide your financial planning whether you decide to pick and choose your own investment or hire expert advice.

1. How much risk am I comfortable taking?

   When can you take risks, and when should you play it close to the chest? Younger investors have time to ride out the dips if the stock market falls. But people with money have more cushioning, too.

2. Why do I need the investment?

   Do I want to save for retirement in the future? If you have time and won't need the cash immediately, you can afford to invest in stocks or mutual funds that have traditionally paid out more for investment but may rise and fall.

   If you need your money to provide a steady source of income, then putting it all in stocks probably isn't a good idea. Do you have to safeguard your nest egg, no matter what, or can you risk losing ground for a little while for bigger gains? If you can't afford any risk, then go for the safety nets like Treasuries, bank CDs, or even a traditional savings account. The point is, knowing how and why you'll need your money is vital to deciding how to save and invest it.

3. When will I need the money?

If you have to cash in at three months, a risky invest-ment is a lousy idea, because you have no time to earn back your money if the market tanks. But a three-month CD, for example, can earn you more than a savings account without jeopardizing your cash.

4. Do I have other sources of money, savings, or income? Will there be anything left over in case the investment bottoms out?

This is where that old adage, "Don't put all of your eggs in one basket" applies.

5. How much do I know about the investment I'm about to make?

It's okay to want to do things the easy way, but don't be dumb. Know the basics and ask questions. After all, you wouldn't hand over your money to your pal, slick Vinnie, to invest in some "hot new deal" without knowing more about it. Why would you give all of your savings to a broker named Victor who has a "sexy little mutual fund" to sell?

Diversity. It's Not Just a Cultural Phenomenon

Diversity is the name of the game. When you own a mix-ture of investments, you spread your risk. How you divide up your investments depends on your financial needs, your stomach for risk, and your total assets. But it's important to note that most experts advise you to diver-sify your assets.

QUICK ⚬ PAINLESS

Are you really, really broke? Then do without one small item a week— say buying lunch or taking a cab. Set aside $10 a week for your future. That's $520 a year. Better yet, have that taken out of your paycheck and invested in your employ-er's 401(k) plan. Your com-pany will also set aside money, and may even match your contribution. That $520 could become $1,040 in a year. Not bad and without much effort!

HIRING FINANCIAL EXPERTS: DO YOU NEED ONE AND HOW DO YOU KNOW YOU'RE GETTING THE BEST ADVICE POSSIBLE?

Once again, it's time to be honest. Will you track your stocks and bonds, read annual reports, attend shareholder meetings, and know as much about investments as possible? Or would you rather spend your days reading courtly love poems under a big oak tree?

If you think you may be a "lazy" investor, then it's best to seek advice from financial planners, stockbrokers, bankers, and personal financial advisors. But keep in mind, even though they look similar in their conservative suits and polished shoes, they're not all the same.

Financial advisors/planners (sometimes called investment advisors) are the people to see to help you plan what you do with your money today and what you'll have or spend in the future. A good advisor is thorough and will go over all aspects of your financial life. Some can help manage your assets. Of course, you'll pay for services either in flat fees or based on a percentage of what you have.

If you're not sure where to find an advisor, start with a professional group.

The National Association of Personal Financial Advisors can provide a list of experts in your state and will mail you a tip sheet on hiring experts. Call (888) 333-6659 or log onto the group's website: www.napfa.org.

Brokers can tell you which stocks, bonds, or mutual funds to buy and sell. You pay them commissions.

QUICK ⟨■■⟩ PAINLESS

You're willing to save but you don't have the time or interest to keep close tabs on your investmetns. Hire a financial advisor or seek help from professionals. You'll have to pay for the service, but if you hire carefully, you won't have to bother with micromanaging your financial affairs.

Someone from a discount brokerage will charge lower fees and commissions. But you may have to do a little work, like researching and choosing investments. An expert at a full-service brokerage will charge you higher fees and commissions, but you get more research, advice, and hand holding.

Warning! Don't just hire anyone! Ask questions. If someone offers you a get-rich-quick deal or pressures you to buy now, be very careful. You also should hear alarm bells if your broker fails to ask you about your needs—how much risk you're willing to take, why you want to invest, how much of your assets you're willing to spend on a mutual fund. Remember, they may be experts, but they're serving you!

The Securities and Exchange Commission is the agency that oversees brokerage houses, and all brokers must be registered with the SEC. Make sure your broker has a SEC license.

You also should:

- Know how the broker gets paid (by commission or a percentage of assets).

- Be aware of how willing the broker is to take risks (it may be more or less than what you're willing to deal with).

- Ask what kind of experience and training they have.

- Insist on getting confirmation slips when you buy or sell stocks, bonds, or other investments.

- Look for trades you didn't authorize. If you see something you didn't agree to, call your broker immediately.

A COMPLETE WASTE OF TIME

The 3 Worst Things to Do When Investing:

1. Believe that any investment you make is guaranteed. You can choose carefully, but remember there is some risk. The more time you have to let your nest egg grow the better.

2. Think you can get financial advice for free. Brokers charge fees or get paid a percentage of your assets. Know how you'll be charged for that expertise.

3. Put your money in stocks, bonds or mutual funds and never pay attention to how you're doing. Read annual reports when they come in the mail and make sure you've authorized any transaction on your account (such as buying or selling stocks).

Your head is normally in the clouds but you've put yourself on solid ground and spent time learning about the practicalities of basic finance. Reward yourself with a book of love poems, a walk on the beach, a cluster of purple balloons, or something just as frivolous.

The Lazy Way

If that doesn't work, you can contact the SEC at 450 Fifth St. NW, Washington, DC 20549, (800) SEC-0330. Or log onto the agency's website: www.sec.gov.

HOW TO KNOW EVEN MORE ABOUT MONEY WITHOUT GOING TO SCHOOL (UNLESS YOU WANT TO)

There are plenty of ways to know about financial markets. You can study like a demon, take the GMAT, and get into business school. If that's too much work and too much money, there are books printed every day on finance, or read magazines and newspapers, such as *The Wall Street Journal*.

Educating yourself about finances can be intensive or casual, expensive or free. Here are a few places to go to learn more about how you can plan a great financial future now that you've mastered the art of eliminating your debts.

- Business school. If you get in and do well, work hard, and genuinely enjoy business, you can get a great job that interests you. But be honest. If you dream of translating ancient Greek war epics so you can earn a coveted tenure spot on a sleepy college campus, then business school probably isn't a great idea.

- Finance courses. If you're in college, why not take a basic business course? You're paying tuition, so you might as well take advantage of your time in school to learn something practical. If you're out of school, that doesn't mean you can't take a course at any of the following:

College extension classes. Most colleges, whether they're four-year universities or city colleges, offer an array of business courses with titles like "Women and Money" to "Everything You Need to Know About Personal Finance." At Rutgers University Cooperative Extension in New Jersey, for example, students can enroll in Money 2000. The purpose of the program is to help students save $2,000 or get rid of $2,000 in debt by the year 2000.

Community Centers. Places like local YWCAs and YWHAs often offer enrichment classes, including courses and seminars on personal finance. The programs are often less expensive than going to a college, and they are usually taught by experts who work in finance.

Visit Wall Street. There's nothing quite like seeing money in action, and if you're ever in New York, skip shopping on Madison Avenue and do your savings a real favor. Go to the city's financial district, arguably one of the most important money centers in the world, and take the following tours:

The New York Stock Exchange Tour: The 45-minute tours are free and self-guided. You'll see a short film on the exchange, learn how stocks are bought and sold, and peer down at the trading floor as stocks are traded. The tours leave continuously from 9 a.m. to 3:30 p.m. Monday through Friday. Get in before noon to make sure you get one of the free passes

QUICK ⬤ *PAINLESS*

Have a few questions about the stock market? Confused about the annual report that arrived in the mail. Try to get a friend who's business savvy to answer your questions in exchange for something you can do, like teaching them to string a tennis racquet or swing dance. You'll help each other learn, and it won't be as dull as reading a financial textbook.

for the tours. Tickets are given out in front of the NYSE at 20 Broad St.

If you have additional questions about the tour, call (212) 656-5168.

If you can't get to Manhattan, visit the NYSE website at www.nyse.com. It has information like stock quotes for the pros. But its education link has great graphics, easy-to-understand explanations on everything from the history of the exchange to how a stock is traded, how stocks gain and lose their values, how to read those abstruse stock tables you see listed in the newspapers, and more.

The Federal Reserve Bank Tour. This isn't just any bank. The Federal Reserve, and its 12 banks nationwide, control the nation's money supply and set monetary policy. Interest rates are controlled by the Federal Reserve Board (the head of which is that fellow Alan Greenspan, the only man who can make a room full of politicians stop talking and listen).

The Fed banks often host free seminars on finance and investing. They are a great, free resource from a reputable, objective agency and well worth attending. (The Boston Fed hosts seminars on understanding the risks of mutual funds as well as fall workshops for National Consumers Week. Call (617) 973-3511 for those Boston events.)

Tours also are available at the Federal Reserve banks nationwide. Stop by the banks' interactive media centers, see a short video on how the bank processes

IF YOU'RE SO
INCLINED

Get a subscription to a business publication—preferrably a magazine—and try to read at least three articles from each edition. You can read the articles during your subway commute, while you wait for your clothes to spin dry, or while getting a pedicure. It doesn't have to take much time to bolster your knowledge and reading consistently will keep you abrest of financial news.

cash, or if you're in New York, tour the gold vault and markets area. You must be 16 or older to take the tour. (Sorry, kids.)

The Federal Reserve district banks are located in Boston, New York City, Philadelphia, Cleveland, Richmond, Atlanta, Chicago, St. Louis, Minneapolis, Kansas City, Dallas, and San Francisco.

Look in your local phone book, under Federal Government, for contact phone numbers. Or, if you have access to a computer, log onto the Fed's super website, which has tour, educational, and other information.

The Internet address is: www.bog.frb.fed.us/otherfrb.htm.

Worried your teenagers will spend you out of house and home. Take them for a tour of the stock market or the Federal Reserve. Talk to them about investing, and show them web sites where they can learn more about the market. The family that budgets, saves, and invests together will ultimately build a brighter future.

The Lazy Way

Getting Money on Your Side

	The Old Way	The Lazy Way
Emergencies	$1,000 on your credit card, which charges 18 percent interest	No problem. You have a four-month emergency fund so you don't have to get in debt.
Retirement	$150 shoved under the mattress	Roughly $500,000 thanks to your annual $2,000 investment in an IRA that's earned you 9 percent interest a year since you've been 22 years old
Financial know-how	"I spend, therefore I sink like a stone"	You know enough to invest, save, and make a killing on small-cap funds

More Lazy Stuff

How to Get Someone Else to Do It

DEBT COUNSELING

Debtors Anonymous

This 12-step program offers free support to help those who want to but have been unable to stop spending or get out of debt. The organization's meetings are an invaluable source of confidential, understanding support for anyone who feels that his or her spending is out of control.

There are Debtors Anonymous chapters across the country, and they will be listed in your local phone book. You may also call or write the organization's General Service Board in Massachusetts.

Debtors Anonymous
P.O. Box 888
Needham, MA 02492-0009
(781) 453-2743

National Foundation for Consumer Credit

This national, nonprofit foundation can help individuals or families get out of debt and plan healthier financial futures.

8701 George Ave.
Silver Spring, MD 20910
(800) 388-2227
www.nfcc.org

FINANCIAL PLANNING

American Financial Services Association Education Foundation

If you can't stand the thought of making a budget, the AFSAEF has put a fun, simple-to-use consumer's almanac on the Internet to help "lazy" consumers like you and me organize savings, expenses, and income. Plug in a few numbers—income, pension, life insurance, and so on, and the almanac computer program does all of the calculations to help you create a budget you can stick to. It's fast, fun, and best of all—free.

The Almanac is posted at:

www.pueblo.gsa.gov/cic_text/money.almanac.calmanac.htm

You can also reach AFSAEF at:

919 18th St. NW
Washington, DC 20006
(202) 466-8611

or by its other website:

www.afsaef.org

Consumer Credit Counseling Service

Fees vary, but CCC's trained and certified financial managers, who are affiliated with the National Foundation for Consumer Credit, can help individuals or families manage their money and provide counseling help with debt. CCC counselors also negotiate with creditors who may be pestering you for payments and help you establish debt management plans and monthly payment schedules you can stick to. CCC may be able to get creditors to stop legal action against you, too. There are more than 1,300 nonprofit CCC offices nationwide. Contact:

National Foundation for Consumer Credit
8611 Second Ave., Suite 100
Silver Spring, MD 20910
(800) 388-2227 or for assistance in Spanish (800) 682-9832

National Association of Personal Financial Advisors

You need help managing your money, but you don't know where to start finding someone right for you. NAPFA can refer you to fee-only planners in your state. Call (888) 333-6659 or check out www.napfa.org.

EDUCATION

Fastweb

This computer database lists over 400,000 college scholarships, many of which students can apply for online. Fastweb can match up students with scholarships so they know where they have the best shot at getting financial aid: www.fastweb.com.

Congressional Hispanic Caucus Institute

CHCI will run free financial-aid searches for Hispanic students using its list of more than 200,000 scholarships. Call (800) EXCEL-DC.

CARS, TRUCKS, AND OTHER VEHICLES

AutoVantage

This is a car-buying service that promises to get you the best deal in your area. They'll negotiate with dealerships. They also offer a towing service and maintenance repair. Membership is $69 a year.

Consumers Automotive

A car-buying service based in Fairfax, Virginia, that will track the best deal for you. If you find a lower price, you get a refund. Fees can be as high as $395: (800) WESHOP4U.

Keep in mind that AutoVantage and Consumers Automotive are just a couple of auto-buying services. Look in your local Yellow Pages and find listings for other buying services in your area.

Autocap

Autocap is affiliated with the National Automobile Dealers Association. It conducts third-party mediation between consumers, dealerships, and mechanics: (703) 821-7144.

Center for Auto Safety

This is the watchdog group started by consumer-rights advocate Ralph Nader. If you have questions about a vehicle's safety record, give these guys a call. They'll have up-to-date information about safety problems.

Center for Auto Safety
2001 S St. NW
Washington, DC 20009
(202) 328-7700

National Highway Traffic Safety Administration

It's one thing to buy an inexpensive car, but how much will you end up spending on a clunker? If you don't have time to review consumer reports, you can contact the NHTSA, which is responsible for reducing injuries and deaths from car accidents. NHTSA also issues recalls on unsafe vehicles. You can get results from their vehicle testing program to find out if your dream car will become a nightmare.

NHTSA
400 7th St. SW
Washington, DC 20590
(202) 424-9393
www.nhtsa.dot.gov

TRAVEL

Lowestfare

Lowestfare is an Internet booking service for travelers who want deals on air fare, rental cars, hotel reservations, tours, cruises, and so on. You may book directly online at www.lowestfare.com or call Lowestfare at (888) 333-0440.

Hotel booking agencies buy blocks of rooms, so they can offer discounts. If you don't feel like shopping around for a great rate, consider using their services.

Accommodations Express (800) 906-4685

Express Hotel Reservations: www.express-res.com or (800) 906-4685

MEDICAL

The following Internet sources can get you medical insurance quotes for the best rates:

Quotesmith: www.quotesmith.com or (800) 556-4393

MasterQuote: www.masterquote.com or (800) 337-5433

If You Want to Learn More, Read These

LOANS AND INTEREST RATES

Bank Rate Monitor

Need to compare mortgages, car or student loans, credit-card rates, and savings account interest? Do you have questions on online banking, repairing your credit, or trimming mortgage costs? Bank Rate Monitor tracks financial offers from hundreds of banks, loan officers, and credit-card issuers. You can compare offers if you're shopping for loans of any kind.

The easiest way to reach Bank Rate is via the Internet (www.bankrate.com). By phone, call (561) 627-7330 or write: 11811 U.S. Highway 1, North Palm Beach, FL 33408.

AUTOMOBILES/TRANSPORTATION

The Better Business Bureau Tips on Auto Insurance, New Cars, and Buying Used Vehicles.

The BBB publishes an array of tips to help consumers avoid costly pitfalls, and its auto insurance tips are among dozens of helpful guides you can get for free from the Internet or by writing the nonprofit group. (Publications cover topics as diverse as telemarketing schemes, tax deductions for charitable organizations, child-care services, and health clubs.)

Its auto insurance guide covers everything from different types of vehicle coverage to selecting insurers, and questions to ask your agent before you buy insurance. Its *Do's and Do Not's After an Accident* also will help you from getting into a financial wreck after you've been in a crash.

To get to the auto guides online: www.bbb.org/library/searchBySubject.html

You also may write:

Council of Better Business Bureaus, Inc.

4200 Wilson Blvd.

Arlington, VA 22203

The Complete Idiot's Guide to Buying or Leasing a Car, by Jack Nerrad, Alpha Books.

What Car Dealers Won't Tell You: The Insider's Guide to Buying and Leasing a New Car, by Bob Elliston, Plume Books.

What Auto Mechanics Don't Want You to Know, by Mark Eskeldson, Technews Publishing.

Take Care of Your Car The Lazy Way, by Michael Kennedy and Carol Turkington, Alpha Books.

EDUCATION

The Guerrilla Guide to Mastering Student Loan Debt, by Anne Stockwell, Harper Perennial.

Take Control of Your Student Loans, by Robin Leonard and Shae Irving, Nolo Press.

U.S. Department of Education

The federal agency has a great website with everything you need to know about student loans. It also accepts applications to consolidate loan debt if you're having trouble keeping pace with your education expenses. To call about the consolidation program, dial (800) 557-7392 or write:

USDOE—Consolidation Dept.

P.O. Box 1723

Montgomery, AL 36102

or log onto the Internet:

www.ed.gov/offices/OPE/DirectLoan/consolid.html.

HOME

Complete Idiot's Guide to Trouble-Free Home Repair, by David Tenenbaum, Alpha Books.

Care for Your Home The Lazy Way, by Terry Meany, Alpha Books.

The Complete Idiot's Guide to Buying and Selling a Home, by Shelley O'Hara, et al, Alpha Books.

The Savvy Renter's Kit: Find the Right Place, Negotiate the Best Lease, Deal with Landlords & Agents, Protect Your Tenant's Rights, by Ed Sacks, Dearborn Financial Publishing, Inc.

Tenant.Net

Renters rights vary from state to state, but New York City–based Tenant.net has posted rental laws for 26 states, plus federal housing codes, public housing law, and tenant news for Australia, Canada, and England. That means with a click of a mouse or a keystroke, it's possible to get the City of Kalamazoo housing ordinances, rent guidelines for Manhattan, or items/repairs/cleaning your landlord must pay for so you don't get stuck with the tab.

http://tenant.net/main.html

CREDIT CARDS

Consumer Federation of America:

This watchdog has been a loud voice in getting credit-card issuers to stop giving Americans more than they can spend responsibly. But it also publishes a host of studies to help you avoid costly traps in health care, real estate, insurance, and more. Ask for a publications list. Most reports cost $10.

Consumer Federation of America
1424 16th St. NW
Washington, DC 20036-2211

TRAVEL

Arthur Frommer's Budget Travel:

This magazine veers off on trails other glossies don't. Issues, which can be purchased at most newsstands, have useful articles such as "The Cheapest Places on Earth," "Swapping Apartments: The Wise and Dazzling Route to Free Travel," or "Las Vegas on $0 a Day." If you're too out-of-pocket to buy the magazine, get it online: www.frommers.com/features/.

Cool Works

If you have the time or the inclination, it's possible to cut travel expenses considerably by working as you go. Another great resource for fun jobs is Montana-based Cool Works, which posts openings on ranches, ski resorts, at RV parks, on cruise lines, or state parks.

Cool Works
P.O. Box 272
Gardiner, MT 59030
(406) 848-2380
www.coolworks.com/showme

GREAT RESOURCES FOR A VARIETY OF TOPICS FROM DEBT TO HEALTH CARE

The American Association of Retired Persons

AARP may be a voice for people over 50, but many of its services can help any of us. AARP members order discount mail-order prescriptions, for example. But the group disseminates advice on ways to obtain the best health care, your rights as a consumer, and retirement planning, among other topics. At the very least, look at the AARP site on Managing Your Debts.

AARP
601 E St.
Washington, DC 20049
(800) 424-3410 or www.aarp.org

Consumer Reports

These are the folks who review our cars, appliances, medical insurance, child-care products, and more so we don't waste money and endanger our health. You can order yearly subscriptions to its reports on health or travel or simply order *Consumer Reports* Magazine for the best deals around. Call (800) 500-9760 for special publications.

Securities and Exchange Commission Free and Super-Low Cost Consumer Catalogs on Debt, Finance, and Everything Else

Who knew the SEC would be such a Santa Claus? The agency produces handbooks on topics ranging from consumers' guides to funerals, how to buy a computer, and guides to disability rights, food, children, and money. Books are free or sold for a mere 50 cents. Order by calling toll free (888) 878-3256, weekdays from 9 a.m. to 8 p.m. Eastern Time; by mail, Consumer Information Center, Dept. WWW, Pueblo, CO 81009; or via the Internet: www.pueblo.gsa.gov/misc.htm.

To get to the SEC Toolkit website, log on at www.sec.gov/consumer/toolkit.htm.

DEBT AND FINANCIAL PLANNING

Certified Financial Planner Board of Standards:

This nonprofit organization regulates the financial planning industry. For brochures on choosing a planner who will be best for you, contact the CFPB at 1700 Broadway, Suite 2100, Denver, CO 80290-2101, or call (303) 830-7500; or on the Internet, go to: www.cfb-board.org.

Credit Repair Kit, Third Edition, by John Ventura, Dearborn Financial Publishing, Inc. Chicago, IL.

How to Get Out of Debt, Stay Out of Debt, and Live Prosperously, by Jerrold Mundis, Bantam Books.

Making the Most of Your Money: Smart Ways to Create Wealth and Plan Your Finances, by Jane Bryannt Quinn, Simon & Schuster.

National Center for Financial Education

The NCFE is a gold mine of information on ways to cut debt and manage your money wisely. Its quarterly newsletter, *The Motivator*, is devoted to a subject per issue (such as paying for education) and is filled with loads of practical advice for cutting costs, avoiding scams, and getting out of debt. NCFE sells books on money planning including general guidelines to workbooks for kids, teens, and parents. Other titles include *The Smart Shoppers Guide*; *The Best Buys for Kids*, a trove of information on where to buy bargain clothes and toys; to videos like *Your Money Attitude*.

P.O. Box 34070

San Diego, CA 92163

(619) 232-8811

www.ncfe.org

Surviving Debt, published and written by the National Consumer Law Center, 18 Tremont St., Suite 400, Boston, MA 02108; (617) 523-8089.

MAGAZINES, PUBLICATIONS, AND MORE

If you're serious about learning more about managing your debt, saving, or making the most out of the cash you have now, you should read financial news, especially *The Wall Street Journal*, fairly consistently. There are dozens of finance magazines, too, and most feature regular articles on personal finance and debt. Pick among *Fortune*, *Forbes*, *Smart Money*, *Business Week*, *Worth*, or *Kiplinger's Personal Finance* magazines.

Smart Money Interactive. If you're a pro, you can check out what the Russell 2000 or NASDAQ and other indexes are doing. If you're just learning, take a look at Smart Money's Answer Center, which covers topics such as automobile financing, college planing, insurance, retirement planning, tax guides, debt management, and more: www.smartmoney.com.

The Wall Street Journal Guide series including: *Guide to Planning Your Financial Future*, *Guide to Understanding Money and Investing*, *Guide to Personal Finance*; published by Lightbulb Press. The pocket-sized books deliver spoon-sized bites of useful information so you get a quick, easy, "lazy" education into finance and planning.

MONEY AND YOUR LEGAL RIGHTS

Federal Trade Commission

The FTC may not sound like the most entertaining group of people to get in touch with, but they have invaluable information about your rights as a consumer. Even if you do owe lots, it's illegal for collection agencies to hound or threaten you. Find out about your rights under the Fair Credit Reporting Act and other applicable law. The easiest way to obtain this information is via the Internet (www.ftc.gov) or write the agency at: 6th and Pennsylvania avenues, NW, Washington, DC 20580 (202) 326-2222.

Money Troubles: Legal Strategies to Cope With Your Debt, by Robin Leonard, Nolo Press.

The book includes simple, easy-to-copy sample letters you can mail to creditors and charts to help you map out repayment plans to get out of trouble. Tips also include methods of dealing with wage attachments, collection harassment, and lawsuits.

Public Interest Research Group

PIRG is another source of valuable information on consumer rights and debtors rights. You'll find tips on dealing with credit-reporting agencies, too. PIRG, 218 D St. SE, Washington, DC 20003; (202) 546-9707 or www.pirg.org/consumer/credit.

CHEAP SHOPPING

Buy Wholesale By Mail 1998: The Consumers Bible to Shopping by Mail, Phone, or On-Line, published by Harper Perennial.

Find-a-Sale

This online site can help you track down sales on everything from clothes to housewares in your neighborhood: www.findasale.com. If you don't have a computer, call Find-a-Sale in New York City, (212) 55-SALES.

National Cooperative Business Association

Such a formal name for what it is: a great source of information about co-ops. (No, they didn't die after the sixties!) There are food co-ops, of course, but how about child care or housing? Write the NCBA at 1401 New York Ave., Suite 1100, Washington, DC 20005-2160; (800) 636-6222; www.cooperative.org.

Valuepage

This online coupon service just premiered in 1998. You can download food coupons redeemable at chain supermarkets like A&P, Pathmark, and ShopRite. Coupons don't always make name-brand food items cheaper than generic brands. But it can be a quick source to save on those boxes of Oreos®. If you're not cutting the calories, you might as well cut your expense: www.valupage.com.

If You Don't Know What It Means, Look Here

401(k). Employer-matched retirement plans where what you set aside from your paycheck toward your golden years is matched by your employer. If you work for a nonprofit, you may be able to invest in a 403(b) retirement plan where both you and the nonprofit contribute toward the fund.

Adjusted Balance. One method credit-card issuers determine how much you owe on unpaid balances. With an adjusted balance, interest and fees that you owe will be figured after all of your payments are deducted from your bill. (See also Average Daily and Previous balances.)

APR or Annual Percentage Rate. Interest rate expressed as a yearly amount. (For example, if you have a credit card with terms that call for an 18 percent APR, you'll pay 1.5 percent (18 divided by 12) in interest every month.)

ATM or Automated-Teller Machines. You put a card in, say a prayer, and viola! Out comes money. Be aware that there are all sorts of new fees attached to ATM transactions.

Average Daily Balance. Another way credit-card issuers calculate what you'll owe in total interest and fees. (See also Adjusted and Previous balances.) The interest you pay is based on the average amount you owe in a single billing cycle (20 to 25 days for most banks).

Bankruptcy. People or companies who cannot pay their debts or who are otherwise in too far over their heads financially can declare bankruptcy to seek protection from those debts. Individuals declare bankruptcy by filing Chapter 7, after which their property is sold to pay off debts. Chapter 13 allows you to keep your assets but pay off debt by five years. Farmers who are bankrupt can file Chapter 12.

Biweekly Mortgage. One method to pay off mortgages. Instead of making monthly payments a year, you divide the monthly fee in half, pay every two weeks, and end up making 13 payments a year. This is a great way to save a bundle on your home loan, because it dramatically cuts the time to pay back your debt and therefore reduces total interest payments. Beware of brokers offering to handle your biweekly payments.

Bonds. One source of income. You earn interest for the bond you buy plus the loan you've made by buying the bonds. Some bonds are tax free, like municipal bonds, which are also guaranteed. Other bonds are known as "junk" because they are high-risk but promise wild returns.

CD or Certificate of Deposit. Another form of investment as you save for your future. CDs are loans that you make to your bank for a period of time or "term" that can be as short as six-months or longer. In return for your invested money, you earn interest.

Credit Bureaus. Credit bureaus keep your financial history, known as credit reports, much like your high school counselor who kept records of all your grades. The information is checked by banks or other lenders if you are applying for funds. Landlords and employers also have been known to obtain credit reports from credit bureaus before they offer people a place to live or a job.

Credit Report. Information you'll find on your personal credit report may include your payment history (including late payments or defaults), total credit limits available to you, lawsuit judgments, savings and spending accounts, the name of your employer, and other personal data.

Debit Card. Looks like an ATM card but different. Issued by banks, the card allows you to withdraw funds from ATMs or use it like a credit card to make purchases. Debit cards instantly withdraw the amount of sales transactions from your account, which means it is impossible to "charge" more than what you have now.

Deductible. An item you can subtract from your reported earnings so you can pay less taxes. (Examples include interest on student loans, home payments, children or other dependents, unreimbursed work expenses.) Anyone with a debt should seek potential deductibles to save money on taxes.

Deferment. A period of time or "intermission" in which a student loan does not have to be paid back. Debtors seeking relief from student loans can seek deferments if they meet certain criteria (such as being in school full-time or working for the Peace Corps). See also, Forbearance.

Education IRA (see IRA).

Forbearance. A financial "time-out" usually up to three months in which a debtor does not have to make monthly student loan payments. One must obtain permission from the issuer or their loan for a forbearance. See also deferment.

Grace Period. The time credit-card issuers give you to pay your balance or debts in full before charging late fees and interest. Beware, grace periods do not apply if you carry a balance.

Interest Rate. The amount you pay to borrow money as expressed in percentages. The lower the percentage, the less you'll pay. Interest rates (sometimes called yields) you pay are in sync with the economy. That's why when rates start falling for the 30-year Treasury rate, the general benchmark for long-term interest rates, then you can expect to save more on home loans, car loans, and other interest rates. Put simply, when interest rates fall, it's cheaper to borrow money. When they go up, you'll pay more.

Introductory Rate. AKA teaser rate or Trojan horses if not careful! These are low rates you pay for obtaining things like credit cards but often go up after a fixed amount of time. Of course, if you carry no balance, interest rates do not matter.

IRA or Individual Retirement Account. Exactly what it sounds like. Individuals can contribute up to $2,000 per year and a couple can sock away $4,000 annually toward their retirement years. The money you contribute to your IRA may be tax deductible.

Keogh Plans. Retirement plans for people who are self-employed or freelance by allowing you to contribute income from those activities.

Medigap Insurance. Supplemental insurance to cover items and care not paid for by Medicare, the federal insurance for Americans who are 65 or older.

Mutual Funds. Forms of investments that can be made up of stocks, bonds, or other assets. Mutual funds are run by managers, so you don't have to track each item in your fund portfolio. Not all mutual funds are created equal, and there are many types to choose from.

Portfolio. A nice, fancy word for your total collection of investments.

Previous Balance. The most common method credit-card issuers use to calculate the interest and fees you'll be charged if you are not paying off your full balances when they are due. Not surprisingly, previous balances are a raw deal for consumers because interest and fees are based on what you owe starting from the date of your last or previous billing cycle. That means you'll pay interest for two months worth of charges, even if you paid off some of those charges. (See also Adjusted and Average Daily balances.)

Principle. Base line. Bottom dollar. The amount owed (or invested) not including interest, fees, or other extras. When it comes time to pay debts, the lower your principle, the less you'll pay in total interest charges. Keep this in mind if you're paying off a huge debt, like student loans or a mortgage. Any extra you send in should be credited to the principle, not interest, to get your debt to zero as fast as possible.

Variable Rate. Also called an "adjustable rate." Both terms describe interest rates that rise and fall over time. You'll find variable rates on everything from home loans to credit-card interest.

Time for Your Reward

So you checked out your credit report, balanced your budget, and you've managed to save instead of spend. That's quite an accomplishment! But you did it *The Lazy Way,* so here are some lazy rewards to give yourself as you continue to cut your spending *The Lazy Way!*

Once You've Done This...	Reward Yourself...
Filed your bills	Get a manicure
Ordered your credit report	Order yourself a gift
Started paying off your credit cards	Go to a museum
Paying bimonthy payments	Give yourself a treat twice a month!
Saved a bundle on airfare	Take a tour
Got a scholarship	Read a trashy novel
Bought an efficient shower head	Take a bath with fragrant oils

Once You've Done This...

Got cheaper car insurance

You brown bag your lunch to work

You got five of your friends to
join a gym with you so you could
qualify for membership discounts

Reward Yourself...

Buy a new air freshener

Take yourself out for a dessert on
Fridays or splurge on a meal-to-go

Use the savings on athletic equipment

Index

Now you can do these tasks, too!

The Lazy Way

Starting to think there are a few more of life's little tasks that you've been putting off? Don't worry—we've got you covered. Take a look at all of *The Lazy Way* books available. Just imagine—you can do almost anything *The Lazy Way!*

Clean Your House The Lazy Way
By Barbara H. Durham
0-02-862649-4

Handle Your Money The Lazy Way
By Sarah Young Fisher and Carol Turkington
0-02-862632-X

Care for Your Home The Lazy Way
By Terry Meany
0-02-862646-X

Train Your Dog The Lazy Way
By Andrea Arden
0-87605180-8

Take Care of Your Car The Lazy Way
By Michael Kennedy and Carol Turkington
0-02-862647-8

Keep Your Kids Busy The Lazy Way
By Barbara Nielsen and Patrick Wallace
0-02-863013-0

All Lazy Way books are just $12.95!

additional titles on the back!

Build Your Financial Future The Lazy Way
By Terry Meany
0-02-862648-6

Shed Some Pounds The Lazy Way
By Annette Cain and Becky Cortopassi-Carlson
0-02-862999-X

Organize Your Stuff The Lazy Way
By Toni Ahlgren
0-02-863000-9

Feed Your Kids Right The Lazy Way
By Virginia Van Vynckt
0-02-863001-7

Cook Your Meals The Lazy Way
By Sharon Bowers
0-02-862644-3

Stop Aging The Lazy Way
By Judy Myers, Ph.D.
0-02-862793-8

Get in Shape The Lazy Way
By Annette Cain
0-02-863010-6

Learn French The Lazy Way
By Christophe Desmaison
0-02-863011-4

Learn Italian The Lazy Way
By Gabrielle Euvino
0-02-863014-9

Learn Spanish The Lazy Way
By Steven Hawson
0-02-862650-8